What to look for
in
CORNISH CHURCHES

What to look for
in
CORNISH CHURCHES

H. MILES BROWN

DAVID & CHARLES : NEWTON ABBOT

for Caroline, Felicity and Jonathan

ISBN 0 7153 5884 7

Set in 11 on 13pt Baskerville
and printed in Great Britain
by Latimer Trend & Company Ltd Plymouth
for David & Charles (Holdings) Limited
South Devon House Newton Abbot Devon

Contents

List of Illustrations

PLATES

LINE ILLUSTRATIONS

Preface

The interest of visitors in our Cornish churches does not lessen, but seems rather to increase, and with the influx of yet more holiday makers the numbers of those 'looking round' during the summer is likely to be greater still.

There is plenty of evidence that the characteristics of our Cornish churches arouse puzzlement in the minds of many. Why is there a church here where there is no village? Who are the strange saints who have given their names to the parishes? How old is the building and why are Cornish churches different-looking from those of other counties?

It may well be that those who have lived long in Cornwall are not sure of the answers and do not realise the whole of the interesting stories these places have to tell. Often they are agreeably surprised when items of interest are pointed out and explained, even in a church they have been familiar with all their lives.

Here is the justification of this book, the outcome of a long and close acquaintance with Cornish churches. It will sketch in the background and describe the ebb and flow of the tides of building and restoration, the changes of fashion, the liturgical alterations and so forth which are part of the story of the Church in Cornwall.

Still more to the point, this book will draw attention to the features of interest in each church which visitors may like to see, and, seeing, find for themselves yet other points of significance. We have every reason to be proud of our county churches and to share our pride with others, acknowledging the debt of gratitude we owe to those many parishioners past and present who have so generously given time and money and care to ensure that the surroundings of Christian worship are seemly and beautiful.

My sincere thanks are due to those who have helped in the writing of this book. I confess my dependence upon the standard works on Cornish architecture—as anyone must surely do who writes on these matters—for the architectural descriptions in the Alphabetical List. These works will be found listed in the Bibliography and the reader who desires more detail is referred to them. Acknowledgement is hereby made to the distinguished authors, but occasionally—greatly daring—I have ventured my own opinion as to the dating of various parts of the structures.

I am likewise grateful to the clergy of the diocese and others who have patiently corrected and amplified the draft entries I sent them concerning the items of interest in the churches under their charge. Especially to my friends Canon A. G. Cooke (Secretary of the Diocesan Advisory Committee) and Canon J. H. Adams, so knowledgeable in many Cornish matters, do I owe thanks for their reading of the introductory chapters and for the advice and encouragement they have so readily given.

St Winnow   H. Miles Brown

I

GENERAL

The Building
of the Churches

The churches of Cornwall have succeeded in capturing and retaining something of the peculiar atmosphere and difference that one becomes aware of in crossing the Tamar into the county.

There is a Cornish version of the westcountry spirit, nurtured among the cliffs, the bleak moors, the wooded valleys and the long sea-sought estuaries. Cornwall, even in the twentieth century, displays marks of its Celtic past. When the spinners of tales for the visitors and the romantics have come and gone, there still remain the ancient stone circles, the menhirs, the wayside granite crosses, the traces of the 'old men', the strange Cornish place names, the Cornish character itself to testify to the length of history in these regions and its difference from the English story. Above all there are the churches, where a particular atmosphere makes itself felt as a brooding spirit of ancient sanctity from a long-vanished Celtic past.

In these churches the village life has ebbed and flowed in rich variety. At the font, for nigh on a thousand years, children have been baptised. In the porch they were betrothed, in the chancel made man and wife. At the altar they received grace and blessing. In the churchyard, or in the church itself, they were laid at death. During life it was in the nave they took secular enjoyment as well as sharing in Sunday worship. In the belfry, during sermons and at the annual vestry, national events were brought to their mind. From the pulpit they were exhorted to their simple village duties. Walls and windows were their art gallery and their only lesson book for the heavenly way. The village churches were for so long the very centre of local life, and in many a building is reflected the enthusiasms and apathy of succeeding generations, their inter-parish rivalry, their humour, hopes and fears.

The buildings of any area naturally display in their style something of local conditions. To a great extent material which lay handy was employed in their construction, and only in exceptional circumstances was it brought any distance. Failing suitable stone, for instance, other material was substituted. In Essex, where stone was scarce, timber towers and porches are found, and brick in the walls. Lacking large enough blocks for quoins and facings, towers in East Anglia are often circular and built of flint, which is also used ornamentally in the walls. The grand towers and churches of Somerset owe their existence to the golden local stone, which will yield to the tools of the stonemason and retain the shape he imposes upon it. The churches of mid-Devon display the warm red stone of the district and glow amid the trees of wooded valleys.

The Cornish churches, too, were fashioned from the material which lay to hand and they reflect the different kinds of stone available in the particular region in which they stand. For, small though the county is, it presents strong contrasts within its circumscribed area. A rocky, spiny ridge of granite outcrops occurs along the central axis, from which the land slopes more or less gently to the north and south coasts. Here and there are deep river valleys. On the north, the Camel, Gannel and Hayle estuaries are wide and sandy, treeless, but bounded not far off by high, forbidding cliffs.

The southern coast is deeply indented by the estuaries of the Tamar and its subordinate, the Lynher, or St Germans river, the two Looes, the Fowey and the Fal with its great harbour and tributary creeks. Some of the valleys are quiet and tree-lined, the roaring winds of winter sweeping over them with little harm. There are granite or slaty cliffs on the north, worn down to knife edges murderous to ships in old days. There are high tors with outcrops of granite boulders softened by bracken and sheep-cropped grass. The south-eastern parts are softer and wooded, rich agricultural areas more steadily prosperous than the areas of speculative mining.

These varying circumstances have had their influence on the church buildings. In the far west and on the north coast they crouch low against the ground, often with squat towers to avoid the western gales. At Tintagel even the very headstones need buttresses to support them against the wind. In the lusher central parts and in east Cornwall where farming was prosperous the towers soar to the heights of Probus or Linkinhorne, St Stephen or Lanlivery, while the churches are wide and graceful.

The chief building materials employed are the slaty greenish stones from Tintagel and the Tartan Down quarry near Liskeard; the Ventergan (Fentrigan) stone from the Warbstow district, Pentewan, near St Austell; Polyphant and the grey stone from Lewannick quarries; moor granite and later in a few places quarried granite, and finally the dark blue catacleuse from the quarry near St Merryn; this last, used occasionally since Norman times, was employed more widely in the latest building phases for detailed ornamental work.

Timber, though once more plentiful than at present, would be neither ample in quantity nor large in dimensions, but the oak sufficed for the curved rafters or principals of roofs, for the carved screens, the bench ends and the like. Mahogany became a fashionable wood for furnishings, pulpits and so forth in mid-Georgian days. Only in the last century did the pitchpine invasion begin to oust the native oak, and it was perhaps the vast quantity of wood imported for the mines from the Scandinavian countries which suggested this distressing material in its shiny profusion.

The distribution of wealth is another deciding factor in the kind of building possible in any area. In a county such as Cornwall, with the Duchy and monastic corporations taking wealth out of the countryside, few families existed with the means to erect great structures such as the wool churches of East Anglia. Many Cornish churches reflect the poverty of the district and places such as Warbstow, Warleggan, Tresmere, Towednack and St John are small and obviously inexpensive. Some are mere moorland chapels. Where there was a sufficiency of means, a great family like the Arundells would lavish gifts and endowments, as we see in their great church at St Columb. Henry Trecarrel turned from his home-building to create such superb structures as St Mary's, Launceston, and the towers of Linkinhorne and St Ive, which traditionally are acknowledged to him. But munificence of this kind is rare in Cornwall.

A peculiar feature of Cornwall, as of Wales and Brittany which share a common background, is the placing of many of the churches. There are those which are remote from the present-day centres of population, or indeed from any medieval village. They are to be found standing alone on windy moorland slopes, down by the river's edge or nestling in some lonely valley. In very few parishes does the traditional English community of manor house, church, parsonage, village green and inn appear with the houses of the community gathered around. The typical Cornish 'churchtown', as the neighbourhood of the church is called, is often no more than a couple of cottages and some-times not even that, while the population lives in hamlets and villages 'way across the parish.

This unusual and sometimes inconvenient placing of our churches is due in many cases to the Celtic origin of the Christian community in Cornwall, on which foundation later ages built. Exactly when the faith was brought to this part of the world is not known. Possibly traders, soldiers in Roman garrisons or other travellers first came with the gospel. Cer-tainly, however, by the fourth century AD there were small isolated groups in the west owning allegiance to Christ, notably in the Hayle area where several very ancient carved stones attest to an early Christian settlement. Eventually a kind of Celtic fringe in Wales, Ireland, Cornwall and Brittany de-

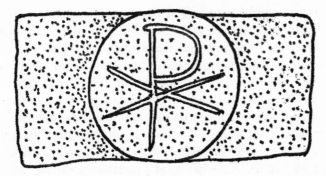

Chi-Rho stone, Phillack, fifth century

veloped a Christian culture, and journeyings among the Celtic lands and beyond were frequent. A series of 'invasions' by Celtic Welsh and Irish priests and by missionaries of both sexes helped the nascent Church to extend and consolidate its hold upon the Cornish converts.

This Celtic form of Christianity formed a bond between tribes and regions left in a vacuum after the Roman legions had been recalled ere the Saxons and others began their incursions. It was an individualistic religion, highly ascetic, demanding extreme self denial and as such evoking the respect and admiration of the Celts. Stories and legends abound of the practices of the Cornish 'saints', their miracles and their influence over animals. Most of these stories are no more than fairy tales, entertainment devised for the winter evenings round the fire for the emulation of the faithful and the satisfaction of parochial pride. Nevertheless, something comes through the multiplicity of stories, and the loyalty of the primitive Cornish was soon given to these enthusiasts.

The Celtic Church had neither parochial nor diocesan organisation; it centred on the monastery. The missionary priest planted his cross, perhaps of wood at first, as a preaching station near the water's edge where he had landed from his coracle up the estuary. Here he marked out his sacred enclosure or 'lan', here his oratory of wood or wattle thatched with reeds may have been built, and then the rough stone huts for his students, who came to learn from him the way of prayer and devotion. In due time converts who wished to lie near their mentor in death were allowed burial in the 'lan'. Here, perhaps, was the origin of our parish churches and churchyards.

Thus Celtic foundations are very frequently on the border of, or not far from, the rivers or streams. Such churches as Ruan Lanyhorne, Gunwalloe, Landulph, Mylor, St Gluvias, St Winnow, St Just-in-Roseland, Kea, St Anthony-in-Roseland and many more of Celtic origin remind us of this by their situation.

It seems clear that at first little building was deemed necessary—perhaps the erection of a cross and the placing of a wooden altar when required in the open air sufficed for the few and scattered Christians in their tiny communities. But inclement weather and other circumstances would demand the erection of a shelter at least for the officiant, while the congregation stood unprotected. Later still, stone buildings for priest and people would arise. Of these later Celtic shrines some fragments survive. They are of rubble, unworked and without any mortar, except possibly clay long since washed away. Such a survival is found on the island of Tintagel, where traces remain of a Celtic religious community or 'monastery' which existed from the fifth to the eighth centuries; the buildings are rectangular and the oratory or church contains its stone altar.

The better-known oratory of St Piran, in the sands north of Perranporth, may possibly date from the lifetime of that 'saint' in the sixth century. Again the building, which was long covered by the loose sand which winter winds pile up, is rectangular, with a doorway on the south side and an altar against the east wall. This doorway was ornamented with crude stone heads and a herring-bone pattern facing, but this may well have been a later adornment. The oratory, which was surrounded by other small buildings belonging perhaps to a community, was abandoned when another church was erected nearby to avoid the encroachment of the sand; this church in its turn was overwhelmed and most of its structure was re-erected some three miles away in a safe part of the parish. The oratory, although now protected by a hideous modern concrete covering, still evokes some faint memory of the pioneer saints, their work and self-denying lives so influential towards the conversion of the Cornish.

The petty princedoms of Cornwall were increasingly threatened by the incursions of the Saxons, who were nominally converted to the Christianity of the vigorous continental Augustine. By the opening of the ninth century Egbert had made a raid through Cornwall and put the inhabitants under tax. The advancing power of the Saxons was such that in or about 840 Kenstec, then bishop-elect of the Cornish, whose seat was in the monastery of Dinurrin, probably Bodmin, submitted to Ceolnoth, Saxon Archbishop of Canterbury. The Celtic Church thus came under the influence of a more vigorous and less provincial form of Christianity, and its peculiarities were gradually discouraged and subdued. King Athelstan in 931 set up a bishopric of the normal diocesan sort at St Germans, with Conan as first bishop; this bishopric lasted until 1042, when the see was united with Crediton and later removed to Exeter. Cornwall remained a mere region, an archdeaconry in the huge diocese of Exeter, until 1876 when the diocese of Truro was founded.

The Saxons probably began that process which divided up the land into manors and parishes. The coming of the Normans merely accelerated the pace of the reorganisation. So many shrines and oratories were associated with the Cornish saints that only about one-third were selected as centres for the new parishes. The rest became places of popular pilgrimage, chapels-of-ease or private chapels on the estates of the new lords.

There is very little in the way of building which can be clearly attributed to the Saxon supremacy. The west end of St Germans church, so obviously Norman in character, displays some more ancient masonry in the interior, and it is possible that this may be part of the old Saxon cathedral. Some few fonts, such as that at Morwenstow, may also antedate the Conquest.

The arrival of the Normans eventually transformed the building scene. At first their preoccupation seems to have been with the greater churches, but by the opening of the twelfth century the oratories and churches in the Celtic and Saxon villages were being rebuilt or furnished in the style familiar to the Norman overlords and enlarged to a size more suited to the increased population and to the dignity of the new church ways.

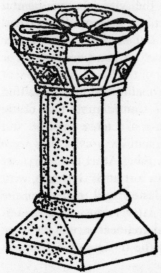

Pillar piscina at Bodmin, Norman

Something like two-thirds of the two hundred-odd ancient churches of Cornwall show traces of Norman work, and this is evidence that some sort of building has stood on the site since at least that time. The churches then erected were usually cruciform, with nave and chancel forming the main axis, and two transepts, narrow in width, forming the minor. Walls are usually about three feet thick, of coursed stone, with joints gradually becoming less coarse as skills advanced. The well known features of round-headed windows and arches obtained in Cornwall as elsewhere. Examples may be seen at St Germans, North Petherwin, Lelant, St Breward, Morwenstow and other places. The Norman doorways had rings of carved stone—'orders' —in diminishing size down to the actual door opening, flanked with quarter-round pillars and capitals. These also can be seen in several places in the county: Landewednack, South Petherwin, St Cleer, Cury, St Martin-by-Looe and Kilkhampton.

A few larger churches had lean-to aisles, and the round pillars of the arcades supporting the main walls were built up of coursed stone—no granite was yet used, as existing tools could not work it. The capitals were of a square or round 'cushion' shape, with ornament on the lower edges of chevron and billet or similar form. Towers could be at the transeptal position, as at Bodmin, or in a central point over the crossing, as seems likely once at Tintagel and at Crantock, but the west end, as with the old tower at Liskeard, was a usual situation; this of course was even more common later.

The Normans, who had large supplies of labour available among the conquered serfs, did import a certain amount of stone from the quarries at Caen, or those at Beer in Devon, but mostly they employed what lay to hand from Cornish sources.

The finest example of the architecture of this period in Cornwall is at St Germans, where a considerable part of the present building displays a Norman character in spite of later additions and nineteenth-century meddling. The west front especially is a splendid spectacle, with its great west doorway of seven orders flanked by two towers, the bases of which are clearly Norman up to the level of the bell stages. Round-headed windows are included in the upper part of the front. The piers and arches supporting the towers within the church and part of the arcade are also from this period, about 1150–60 AD. The whole of this church repays close study.

By far the most frequent survival from Norman times is the font. In many churches this is the only remaining evidence that the Normans erected a building at the spot, so completely obliterating have later rebuildings been. Of the fonts of this period the most splendid example will be found at Bodmin, where it stands as one of the clearest examples of Norman skill. The bowl is circular, with a square brim. There is a central supporting shaft surrounded by four subsidiary pillars at the corners, the upper parts being fashioned into angel heads. The sides of the bowl are deeply undercut with vigorous emblematic figures and grotesques. The material used is the grey stone from Lewannick parish. Of this type of font several other examples, though not so fine, can be found at St Austell, St Columb Minor, St Cuby (Tregony), St Ewe, Kea, St Stephen-in-Brannel, St Stephens-by-Saltash. Other fonts are of a simple bowl shape ornamented with bandings; such a one may be found in the nineteenth-century church at Herodsfoot, having stood at one time in the chapel at Respryn in the parish of St Winnow. Other Norman fonts are square with panelled sides, and yet others are of individual pattern.

Interesting tympana—the semi-circular space between a round-headed arch and the square top of the door it surrounds—carved with symbolic figures remain. Egloskerry church has two; the north doorway displays a fearsome beast, the south the Agnus Dei, or Lamb and Flag. At Rame the tympanum has three circular motifs, and at Tremaine the tympanum is now mutilated as a result of a nineteenth-century stove pipe having been put through it! The Agnus Dei also appears at St Michael Caerhayes on the Norman tympanum of the north door.

Another period of activity in church building, though interrupted by times of war, apathy and plague, occurred in the thirteenth and fourteenth centuries. By then the Norman churches were as old fashioned and dark as in their turn the Saxon ones had been. The graceful, slender thirteenth-century lancet windows, the slighter columns put in when aisles were added gave a lighter effect, and the more pointed windows and arches relieved the sense of heaviness. Where aisles were added the original Norman transepts would be absorbed and the cruciform plan obscured, but additional room and the opening of vistas were compensations. An original cruciform plan church of the thirteenth century can be seen at St Ervan. Western towers were commenced on a wider scale, and the lower stories of not a few Cornish towers date from this time, among them the tower and spire of St Enodoc, the example at Sheviock and the lower storey at Lostwithiel.

So great was the building activity that in the high summer of 1259 the bishop of Exeter, Walter de Bronescombe, made a tour of the county and dedicated some nineteen parish churches

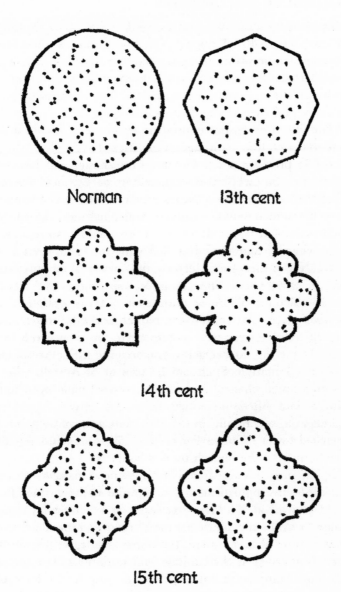

Norman

13th cent

14th cent

15th cent

Common pier sections

which had been rebuilt or remodelled. Among them St Breoke, St Anthony-in-Roseland, Sheviock and others retain considerable features from this time, but most have been so largely rebuilt that little survives. Good fourteenth-century work remains at St Ive, in the chancel, sedilia, niches and piscina, and in the window tracery at Sheviock.

The fifteenth century is pre-eminently the period of intense activity in church building. Many must have fallen into disrepair in previous years, but new enthusiasms and new ideas demanded the wholesale remodelling of existing structures whatever their condition. Nearly every church in Cornwall was altered or added to in this century, which left them pretty much as we see them now. Many remaining narrow Norman aisles were widened and roofs installed with the same span as the nave. New aisles were thrown out where none previously existed, windows of three, four or more lights and delicate tracery, slender pillars of granite—the main section in one massive piece—flatter four-centred arches with wider spans, and splendid towers were commenced, the new work being grafted on to the older structures on occasion with makeshift and obvious adaptation. Such can be seen at St Austell, where a Norman aisled chancel and chantry chapel have been linked with a late fifteenth-century nave and tower. St Mary's, Launceston, was rebuilt in the early sixteenth century, but the detached tower of an earlier church still stands and was once separated from the church by two cottages.

By the time this active period commenced masons' tools had become more sophisticated, and granite in its various forms could be worked. The two arcades at St Veep display the advance in skill—the south arcade is crudely formed of moorstone granite of about 1340; the north arcade, built a century later, is adorned at the capitals with floriations far more skilfully cut. Many beautiful ornamented items in the dark blue catacleuse stone, from the quarry and workshop at St Merryn, begin to appear more widely from the early fifteenth century onwards. The reredos at St Issey, the shrine at St Endellion and the tomb of Prior Vyvyan at Bodmin are among the many examples of Cornish skill in this material.

In spite of the wholesale remodelling of churches at this period, the plan of lean-to aisles with a clerestory, or line of windows in the nave wall above the lean-to roofs, survived. At St Germans, Callington, North Petherwin, Lostwithiel and Fowey examples can be seen. These last two have arcades of similar construction, the pillars sweeping into the arches without capitals. The influence of foreign architects may be responsible for this unusual design.

The late fifteenth and early sixteenth centuries mark the close of the effective era of medieval building. The peak of accomplishment may be seen in such examples as the elaborate and masterly treatment of granite in the tower of Probus. This shows such likeness to the great towers of Somerset that it surely implies an architect familiar with that style but adventurous enough to use granite instead of the softer Somerset stone. This Probus tower was not completed, owing to a dispute concerning the quarry, until at least the reign of Mary. Similar elaboration in ornamentation of the structure can be seen at St Mary's, Launceston, St Mary's, Truro, and the tower at St Austell, as well as in individual features in other churches, standing as evidence of the masons' fully developed skills and the range of architectural ideas.

A peculiar and late feature of some west Cornish porches is the tracery in the arch of the outer doorway, as at Mylor. In the Lizard district a very local style characterises the churches. One feature of those at Landewednack, Cury and St Mawgan-in-Meneage is the squint at the junction of chancel and south transept. One or more pillars with arches support the upper part of the corner, and the passageway is covered outside by a diagonal wall with a small window to provide light. Another peculiarity of far western churches is the small arch between the arches of the arcades, which seems to have some connection with the roodscreen. This will be found at Paul, Wendron and elsewhere.

The evolution of the Cornish church was thus a gradual process, with local variations, additions and alterations in the prevailing style of the period. No two buildings are exactly alike and every one is worth examining in detail to see the steps by which it attained its form, practically the present-day form except for minor additions such as vestries and the like.

Of course, not all churches were completed according to a developed plan, and all show individualities in construction. A parish may have been too poor or too small to erect two aisles and would be content with one, normally the south aisle. But in some cases the north aisle was built instead, as at Budock, St Erney, Botus Fleming, Quethiock, Morval, St Keyne and Duloe. Perhaps a short aisle or chantry on one side as well as an aisle of full length on the other would be erected. At Lansallos and at Ladock the short aisle is on the north, while at Liskeard the short south aisle is added to the normal one, as it is also at St Ives. A wealthy family might add as a particular feature its own chapel or chantry in a style different from that of the rest of the church. The Colshull chapel at Duloe has two bays of Caen stone pillars, deeply cut with vines and foliage, which is among the best late fifteenth-century work in Cornwall. The great Arundell family, one of the richest in medieval Cornwall, left many traces of its beneficence in the church structure at St Columb.

Many of the noteworthy towers in the county date from this time. Some, like Probus (the highest in Cornwall, at 125ft 10in), Lanlivery, Linkinhorne, St Buryan, Stratton, North Tamerton, soar to a tremendous height, several being ornamented with bands of granite at the base carved with trefoils, panels and crosses. In the far west the towers are more usually stumpy and without buttresses, as at Zennor, Sennen and Landewednack. At the last, blocks of serpentine, the local stone, give a pleasing effect to the building.

In a few places the towers stand apart from the church. At Gwennap the tower with a conical roof houses a peal of bells

Tower buttress, St Wenn, fifteenth century

and is near the churchyard gate, very convenient for non-churchgoing ringers! Lamorran, Feock, Mylor and Gunwalloe towers are small and without feature. At Talland the tower is attached to the church by a passage, and part of it is cut from the living rock. The church at Illogan was rebuilt a little way off from the medieval site, leaving the tower to stand by itself.

The typical Cornish tower is of three stages (a few, like Towednack, are of two). The lowest opens into the church with a tall arch and has a west door and window; the next stage is merely a small room under the bells, with diminutive windows, and the bell stage itself contains the cage for the bells—usually but three at this date—and windows on each face with slate or stone louvres or slate slabs perforated to let out the sound of the bells. Occasionally one of these belfry windows may be omitted to prevent the driving rain entering, as at Morwenstow where there is no west window on the belfry stage.

The tops of the towers are frequently adorned with pinnacles at each corner, and these are in many instances, like the Devon examples, of considerable size. There may be a stair turret up one side or at one corner, as at St Buryan and St Stephen-in-Brannel. Sometimes this turret terminates in a spirelet, as at St Columb Major, St Allen and St Mawgan-in-Pydar. In the towers of St Blazey, Lanlivery, Luxulyan and Linkinhorne the great squared blocks of granite in the structure are very striking. Occasionally, where medieval houses crowded the church, the necessity of a processional path round the building would be met by open arches at the base of the tower. This arrangement survives at St Columb, and may be discerned also at St Blazey and Lostwithiel, though later vestries have blocked one arch in these two churches.

Rural granite, St Winnow, fifteenth century

Unlike some counties, Cornwall is not rich in spires. There are in fact fewer than twenty, including modern examples, but no clear reason for this dearth appears. Several ancient spires are found near the north coast as well as the south, so a fancied inability to resist the winter storms is not a factor. The spires of St Enodoc, St Minver, Cubert and St Agnes all stand near the coast on the north of the county, and St Keverne, St Hilary, Gerrans, St Anthony-in-Roseland, St Ewe, Sheviock and Rame are not far from the coast along the southern border. Inland are the spires of Menheniot and the lantern and spire of

Lostwithiel, with an octagonal traceried story of design unique in the county. A few of the towers along the north coast were recognised landmarks for shipping, and one (St Eval) was later rebuilt partly at the expense of Bristol shipping merchants, whose ships it helped to navigate before the erection of the Trevose lighthouse. At Maker in the eighteenth century the tower was a recognised signal station for the navy and a copy still survives of the signals flown from the top.

The churches in Cornwall are thus seen to display a strongly regional character, with local variants in the material used, in their disposition and in the craftsmanship involved. By more sophisticated standards they are often crude and homely, but the result is a clear evocation of the Cornish spirit and atmosphere.

From the late sixteenth century the exterior of the churches remained comparatively unaltered. The eighteenth century added its sundial to the porch, the nineteenth its memorial clock in the tower. The period since has filled the churchyard with the white of quarried granite headstones and kerbs, detracting from the dignified lines of the old church, which had been content to live with the slate headstones of former epochs.

Within, however, much of the scene is different from that which was familiar to the medieval builders, though often enough remains for us to recapture something of the colour and glow and mystery of the fifteenth-century interior.

As is still frequently seen, the roof inside is almost a semicircular, slightly pointed, barrel-like structure, stretching the whole length of the nave and chancel with similar roofs over each aisle. It is framed with curved principals and horizontal purlins, which divide the whole into rectangular panels. At the crossings of the timbers carved bosses are fixed, which often display emblems and grotesque forms. The under surfaces of the roof timbers are often moulded or carved, while the feet of the principals, where they meet the wall plate, are sometimes hidden by carved angels holding shields. All this woodwork would have been picked out in bright colours, of which some traces remain. Over the junction of chancel and nave the ceiling —chancel arches are rare in Cornwall—often has extra ornament, as at this point it ran over the figures of Christ and his attendants mounted on the roodscreen, which every medieval church possessed.

A considerable number of these screens remains in the westcountry and Cornwall possesses some excellent examples, in which the native craft reveals its unsophisticated approach and sometimes crude workmanship. At St Buryan the screen's cornice depicts a scene of evil being hunted out by good. Lanreath has a traceried screen with its lower panels displaying paintings of saints. Painted lower panels remain at Budock and at St Winnow they are carved in bold patterns. At St Mawgan-in-Pydar the lower parts are open without either panels or tracery. Good restored screens can be found in position at St Ewe, Laneast and Altarnun, and fragments remain in other parishes. The traditional figures of the rood, Mary and John, were universally destroyed in the troubles of the sixteenth century; where they appear today they are replacements in the ancient style, and some modern screens, as at Blisland, try to reproduce the colour and form of the older construction. Between the chancel and the chancel aisles parclose screens, simpler but of similar pattern, would be erected.

The wide loft at the top of the screen is supported by coved wooden vaulting; it was used, among other purposes, by the attendant who kept the light burning before the rood. It is possible that singers and small organs were placed there. Access to the loft was gained by stairs in the thickness of the wall and openings in the arcades above the piers. In many places where the screen has vanished these stairs and openings can be seen, to the mystification of many. At St Keverne there are no less than three sets of roodloft stairs at various points along the wall—a mystery no one has as yet satisfactorily solved.

Originally these screens, like the roofs, would have been

aglow with colour. They served the purpose of dividing the nave, which was used for secular purposes such as church ales, as well as for the congregation at worship, from the chancel and chapels. Within the screen would be perceived the high altar and the subsidiary altars of the chantries or guild chapels. Many references to bequests to parish guild altars remain in Cornish wills of the period.

Until the introduction of seats in the churches, which in Cornwall might be in the later part of the fifteenth century, the congregation stood or knelt on the rush-strewn floor. The pews and benches which remain, and the far greater number of bench ends which survive, now married to Victorian pitch-pine seats, display such a wealth of craftsmanship and imagination in their carved subjects as to furnish a study in themselves. Most date from the late fifteenth or early sixteenth century, but there are some, as at St Winnow, from the seventeenth century, and these show the continuance of the craft in spite of religious changes. The pilgrim at St Levan, the jester and grazing sheep at Altarnun, the wind-tossed ship at St Winnow, and the mermaid at Zennor are subjects frequently photographed. The carved borders are typical of Cornish work: occasionally, as at St Minver, Talland and St Ives, there are kneeling figures carved on the top as a finial or 'poppy head'.

On the walls frescoes were painted in crude colour and perspective. A favourite subject was St Christopher carrying the child Jesus. Another in Cornwall was the Christ of the trades—the Lord surrounded by implements used in daily life. Such wall paintings—greatly restored—can be seen at Breage, Poughill, Linkinhorne and a few other places.

In the windows stained glass continued the teaching by eye. St Neot boasts a whole range of early sixteenth-century examples—restored, surprisingly, in the early nineteenth century —depicting scenes from the life of the parish saint as the legends had it. Some of these were gifts from the women and men of the day. This range of windows is unique in Cornwall, and unusually fine by any standards. Ancient glass in more or less complete windows may be seen at St Winnow, St Kew and Laneast, and other parishes carefully preserve fragments or parts of windows.

The effect of all this colour was to make the churches bright, in vivid contrast to the primitive conditions in which the parishioners lived. As their local art gallery, their contact with culture, it impressed upon their minds through their eyes the great facts of the Christian faith. Much of this richness was provided by the locals themselves, or those closely kin. The labouring, the fetching of stone, some of the actual masonry and woodwork would be carried out by the villagers. In some cases contracts survive, as at Bodmin, for the seating and screens; there the locals required the craftsman, Matthy More, to produce items similar to those in churches they had visited, only better!

These simple folk of the countryside seldom achieved any lasting memorial after their death. The gentry and richer families, however, sought to make their memory permanent and memorial brasses on which their effigy was engraved became common. Some are still to be seen in Cornwall, though they are not of the quality or quantity found in counties further east. There are, however, several fine ones at St Mawgan-in-Pydar, commemorating members of the wealthy and powerful Arundell family of Lanherne and its branches. Constantine, Quethiock, St Mellion, St Minver, Cardinham, Blisland, St Ives and Lostwithiel also possess interesting brasses. Some of them are 'palimpsests', or re-used brasses, on whose discarded side are sometimes much more ancient reminders of long-dead worthies. From these memorials the details of contemporary costume, armour and the like can be studied.

People of less wealth or simpler taste could be remembered by slate memorials within the church carrying their effigy or similar illustration. The main period for this kind of Cornish slate monument is rather later—the sixteenth and seventeenth centuries in particular. Helland has an early slate memorial to Humfrey Calwodely, c 1500, but most are post-Reformation in date.

The effect of this great religious upheaval on the churches of Cornwall, and how they later fared through times of carelessness and over-enthusiastic restoration up to the present day, demands a chapter to itself.

II

GENERAL

The Sixteenth Century and After

The ecclesiastical realignment of the sixteenth century was borne along on the continuing political crisis of the Henrician succession, which was a catalyst of the unrest of the Church in England. At the heart of the religious changes was a preference for openness rather than mystery; hearing rather than seeing; scriptural rather than ecclesiastical authority; the auditory rather than the theatre as the ideal setting for worship. Between these limits a multitude of opinions prevailed, from the high churchism of some Anglicans to the extremism of those who were influenced by events in continental countries where the Reformation was a revolution and a new beginning. These differing attitudes are reflected in the treatment accorded to the church buildings.

The repudiation of papal authority and the dissolution of the monasteries under Henry VIII left the mass of the people—apart from those whose livelihood depended on the disbanded religious communities—untroubled, if not relieved. In Cornwall at the time of the dissolution these religious communities were small in numbers and run down, and the conservative hand they kept on the affairs of growing towns was resented. But, when the familiar parish services were interfered with under Reformation legislation and the churches rearranged, with the casting-out of things but lately provided and barely paid for, there was opposition and division of loyalties.

In the last years of Henry VIII moderate changes began. In

1545 the Chantries Act ordered the confiscation of chantry ornaments and lands to finance the Scottish war; inventories of parish goods were commenced, but, owing to Henry's death, the order did not come into effective operation until the first years of Edward VI. It prepared parishioners for what was to follow. In the year 1547 images and statues of a 'superstitious' kind were ordered to be removed. This involved the destruction of the rood with its attendant figures; not more than a fragment of any of them survives in the whole country, so thorough was the execution of this order. Certain other ornaments and customs were also forbidden. The Royal Arms began to appear in the churches—in some places actually where the rood had been, though there are no surviving examples of this date in Cornwall.

In 1549 the first English prayer book was issued, and this, together with the changes made in the churches, provoked a rebellion throughout the southwest which was only crushed by the use of foreign mercenaries; the demands of the rebels included the restoration of the services as they were in King Harry's day, and one reason given was that Cornishmen did not understand the English tongue. It is interesting that the rebels did not require the resumption of papal authority and communion with Rome. In the savage reprisals which followed, the bells of the churches, except the smallest, were ordered to be removed. As it happened, only the clappers were taken—and these were easily replaced!

Under the more vigorously protestant régime of Edward's council the old stone altars were removed (1551) and wooden tables introduced to stand in the nave or lower chancel for the communion. One such table said to date from this reign survives at Poughill. The second Edwardian prayer book, 1552, hardly came into use in the far west, but the delivering up of the plate and jewels of the parish churches ordered in 1553 was well in hand and the Cornish plate actually on its way to London when the young king died and Mary came to the throne.

Under Mary the plate was handed back to the parishes, and the old order briefly resumed. Stone altars were re-erected, the rood was replaced—sometimes only on painted canvas, so sceptical were the parishioners as to the permanence of the régime. There was much finishing-off of woodwork, pews, pulpits and the like begun just before the breaking of the storm. The pulpit at St Mawgan-in-Pydar and the bench ends at Kilkhampton date from this time and the tower at Probus neared completion.

The brief and bitter reign of Mary did not permanently arrest the Reformation tide. Indeed, on her death in 1558, the return of exiles who had fled from her persecutions brought more decided protestant opinions, learned from sojourns in Frankfurt, Zürich, Geneva and elsewhere. Queen Elizabeth sought a middle way, and when the Anglican position found a justification for itself and men settled down to its ways, craftsmanship began to flourish again. The Marian stone altars, where they existed, were taken out once more, it is true, but sheer destruction was deprecated and the Elizabethan and later furniture was of more seemly proportion and workmanship than Edwardian makeshifts could have been. Elizabethan communion tables of great dignity can be seen at St Martin-by-Looe and Jacobstow, and Lawhitton has a Jacobean one of early date. At Boconnoc is a notable table bearing the inscription 'made by me, Sir Raynold Mohun, 1621'. It is richly carved and of generous proportions, and is still in use.

The Marian rood figures were destroyed by order of Elizabeth's commissioners, who toured each county to see the new régime put into action. The rood figures at Landulph, with the mass books, were burnt at Saltash in 1559; those at Menheniot were sold at Liskeard. The screens, however, remained, though in some places, such as St Winnow, Lanreath and Altarnun, the lofts were removed according to the order of 1561. This order was not enforced rigorously except in puritan areas and some screens remain with lofts in all their beauty (as at St Ewe and St Mawgan). In some places, though not frequently in Cornwall, new screens were erected in Jacobean times where they were lacking. The old screen at Morwenstow is said to have been put up in 1575.

Much woodwork of the early seventeenth century still remains. There are font covers at Lanreath, Launcells and St Winnow. Pulpits exist at St Keverne, Liskeard (dated 1636), Stratton, Lanreath, Marhamchurch, Boconnoc, South Petherwin (dated 1631) and St Winnow. An impressive Jacobean pulpit at Kilkhampton was removed in 1860, but a sketch

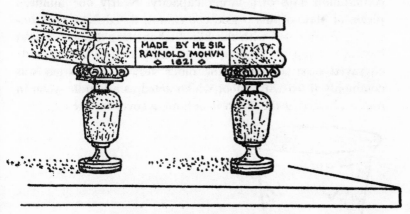

Jacobean communion table, Boconnoc, 1621

remains to show its grandeur. Many bench ends display the characteristics of this period—renaissance patterns of beauty but of no significant or symbolic form like the earlier ones with their passion emblems. Some, however, are graced with simplified symbols such as the diocesan arms of Exeter, the chalice and bread, the crossed keys and so forth at St Winnow. These last date from about 1620, and though simpler than earlier examples, are still fine pieces of workmanship, deeply carved. Parclose screens dated 1612, within which Walter Langdon, a local squire, made himself comfortable, still exist at St Martin-by-Looe.

A good deal of Elizabethan silver communion plate remains

in the county. Only one piece, a paten at Morval, survives of the pre-Reformation possessions of the parishes, although a few places have obtained in later years ancient examples from else-where (as at Antony and St Kea). At Elizabeth's accession in 1558 the old chalices and patens remained in use, but the resumption of communion in both kinds by the laity meant the old ones were too small. There was also a certain amount of dislike of the 'massing cups' by those of puritan mind. An order made about 1574 required their replacement by seemly communion cups of a larger capacity. Nearly one hundred pieces of plate of this period are extant, dated from 1574 on-wards, ornamented with the Elizabethan strap decoration and having a knop or swelling in the middle stem and a wide engraved base similar to the older vessels. The paten was commonly fitted with a foot which acted as a handle when in use; on inverting the paten it became a cover for the cup.

Elizabethan communion cup and cover paten, 1574

Another way of furnishing the Tudor altar was by the gift of domestic vessels, and there are several fine examples of Elizabethan silverware of this kind given by wealthy benefactors. After Elizabeth's order of 1574 little plate was needed for a long time. There are only about ten pieces of James I's reign and about fourteen of Charles I's reign. The Commonwealth produced little or no plate: the necessity did not exist for it.

These graceful examples of the art of the silversmith are in use still in some churches, perhaps only on feast days, being on ordinary occasions replaced by modern and less delicate plate designed for present-day custom. But all the ancient plate is securely kept and may be inspected only by special request and appointment at the discretion of the incumbent.

In the 1570s the rapid rise of the puritan party, who desired a more thorough reform of the Church according to their ideas, placed the many survivals of medieval workmanship under suspicion. More ornaments and usages were laid aside or destroyed. The frescoes on the walls were whitewashed (ironically this tended to preserve them for a more appreciative age) and scriptural texts took their place. Pretentious tombs sometimes invaded the seldom-used chancel, replacing the heavenly concern of a previous generation by commemoration of worldly success. Such tombs are found at Lanreath, Mevagissey and Pelynt.

The course of the Civil War in Cornwall involved damage to a few of the churches. The campaign around Lostwithiel in August 1644 brought destruction of the massive tower of St Nectan's chapel in St Winnow parish. It has never been rebuilt, and its truncated form may be seen to this day, with one of the old pinnacles from the top lying in the churchyard. At Lostwithiel the steeple was damaged, the font overturned, the church used as a stable and the roof largely blown off by an explosion of gunpowder.

The ascendancy of the puritan school of thought and church discipline 1646–60 broke the still discernible thread of medievalism. Their—very proper—ideal of grave dignified simplicity in worship often came to be dreary bleakness in practice. There was further destruction of stained windows. Organs—only a few existed in Cornwall—were proscribed. In 1647 the organ and screen at St Ives were broken up. The Launceston organ was taken down and stored for happier times. Figures in external niches were dragged down. So familiar did the sight of these empty niches become that nineteenth-century architects designed their buildings with already-empty niches, such as at Lostwithiel vestry (1875)!

Building ceased and churches became ruinous. St Mewan never repaired their tower; it is still shorn of its proper crown. Mevagissey sold its bells to take down its tower rather than repair it.

The legacy of Civil War factions and Restoration parliament legislation was a bitterly divided nation and an impoverished county. It was a considerable time before much restoration and refurnishing of the churches was possible. There was widespread ignorance of and opposition to the working of the Anglican system in some country areas.

However, the new and growing town of Falmouth, close to the castle at Pendennis which had held out so long against parliament forces, was furnished with a church by the express support of Charles II. He had fleetingly stayed at the castle in 1646, and expressed the wish that a church be built for the town. It was founded in 1662 and consecrated in 1665 as a memorial and commemoration of the Civil War in Cornwall. In a style then unique in Cornwall it combined the renaissance and gothic architectural modes. The arcades are of Tuscan columns of granite, while the walls contain windows of the usual late fifteenth-century style. The church, dedicated to King Charles the Martyr, was enlarged in 1684, a chancel being added and a poor tower—missing an opportunity for a much more suitable Wren steeple.

The fashion of building columns of a circular section with capitals vaguely aping a Greek style prompted a new aisle in this form at Crowan, of which a column base from about 1680 remains, and at Pelynt, where a Tuscan arcade can still be seen. Redruth, rebuilt in 1756, is a later example of this style, which remained fashionable for some time and inspired some odd variations.

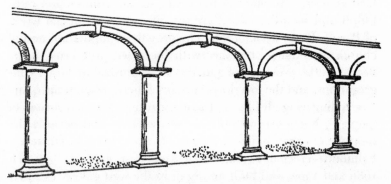

Tuscan arcade at Pelynt, seventeenth century

The general replacing of the altar tables in the chancels after the Restoration also involved the erection of communion rails. The rails at Altarnun, dated 1684, stretch the whole width of the church, and another set, now placed across the tower arch at North Petherwin, is dated 1685. Other parishes, too, were busy with this work. At Breage the rails were put up in 1693; Antony erected them in 1698. By the end of the century it was unusual for the altar table to be without rails, and in several places part of the old communion rail survives, either in situ as at St Sampson, Golant, St Minver and Rame, or worked up, as at St Endellion, into other furnishings.

These last decades of the seventeenth century witnessed a new enthusiasm for the Church of England. Much refurnishing and enrichment resulted, as well as the formation of religious and missionary societies and the re-commencement of weekday services in addition to the Sunday ones. For a while Jonathan Trelawney, bishop of Exeter 1688–1707, made Trelawne, in the parish of Pelynt, his residence. Some of the chapel furniture there, including a bishop's throne, may be seen at the County

Museum, and a replica of his pastoral staff, borne at his funeral, is still at Pelynt with his chair.

The taste of that age ran to panelling, comfortable pulpits and pews approaching the horse box-type common in the later Georgian era. At Madron the belfry screen, communion rails, pulpit and sounding board are the gift, if not the actual work, of Parson Rowe about 1706. The growth of population and of church attendance, together with increased prosperity, is reflected in the provision of galleries to accommodate larger congregations, and the erection of organs. There was in some quarters a lingering dislike of these instruments as savouring of 'popery', but a greater obstacle was expense and possibly the shortage of organ builders after the Commonwealth. However, Falmouth erected north, south and west galleries between 1686 and 1702, and built an organ in the west gallery in 1702, despite the opposition of the son of the church's chief local benefactor, Sir Peter Killigrew. This must have been the first organ in Cornwall after the Restoration. Galleries at St Mary's, Launceston, St Mary's, Truro, and at Penzance carried organs in 1718, 1750 and 1769. Many churches in populous areas were soon burdened with unsightly galleries for singers, charity and school children and the poor, while the better-class folk occupied spacious box pews at floor level. These galleries have almost all been swept away from the medieval churches, but many buildings still bear traces of them in the mutilations cut in pillars and walls for their support. Galleries still remain at Falmouth, Helston, St John's, Truro, and Torpoint. High box pews can still be seen at Launcells, and similar ones at St Sampson (Golant), Budock and Paul.

Plenty of evidence remains that the interiors of this period were frequently graced with rich hangings of velvet at the altar and pulpit. At Camborne a velvet 'carpet' for the communion table survives. In 1760 Humphrey Mackworth Praed gave a new altar cloth and pulpit cloth to St Uny Lelant. Sir John St Aubyn, fifth baronet, gave his parish of Crowan an altar cloth worth £150. St Ives has a terrier, or list of goods belonging to the church, of 1765 with mention of similar adornments and candlesticks (probably hanging chandeliers) in some profusion. Several churches possess these chandeliers dating from the middle eighteenth century, and they may be seen at St Just-in-Penwith (1746), Helston (1763), Sennen, Paul (1765) and Redruth (1798) among other places, mostly in the far west.

Up to the seventeenth century most churches contented themselves with three bells in the tower as in medieval days; any greater number was a rarity. The coming of the eighteenth century saw an improvement in the control exercised by the ringer over his bell; it became possible to strike the bells in a regular order. Numbers of towers were speedily furnished with rings of five, six or—more rarely—eight bells and ringing became a popular and fashionable art. Between 1712 and 1824 no fewer than eighty-three rings were cast for Cornish churches and in one year alone—1767—six complete rings were hung. Many additional bells and recastings stand as evidence of the enthusiasm for this peculiarly English and Cornish activity, which was then considered to be as suitable for the gentry as for humbler folk. The wealthy 'Squire' Lemon of Truro, and the curate of St Mary's, Rev Samuel Walker, spent much time with other ringers in the belfry at Kenwyn. A great proportion of the eighteenth-century bells in the county bear the name of Pennington, a family of bell founders who worked from Bodmin, Lezant and Stoke Climsland. One member of this family was drowned while taking a bell across the Antony ferry to Landulph church in 1768. His memorial slate is in the Landulph tower. Casting of bells was more usually carried out near the church in whose tower they were to be hung. It was easier, before the better roads of the nineteenth century, to carry the material to the church than to risk the cracking of a bell by transport over rough roads.

The ringers' rules, still to be seen in bucolic rhyme in many a tower (Lanlivery, Calstock, St Endellion), show the efforts made to keep order and attention among the ringers, with fines of sixpence a time—a half day's pay at least—for irreverent behaviour or unskilful ringing.

Charity boards still exist from this century, for example at Liskeard, Probus and St Winnow, recording the gifts made by the wealthier folk for the relief of the poor, and the conditions under which the income is to be shared out. Modern circumstances have caused many of these charities to be commuted in some way, as the original intentions are nowadays impossible to fulfil. At Lostwithiel, for instance, the charity provided that

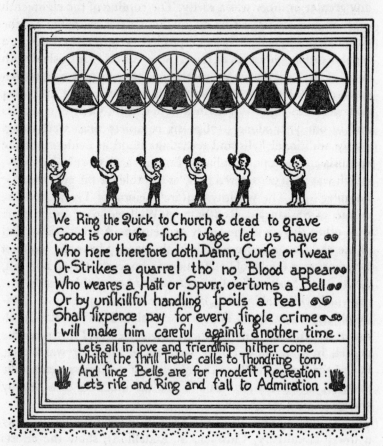

We Ring the Quick to Church & dead to grave
Good is our ufe fuch ufage let us have
Who here therefore doth Damn, Curfe or fwear
Or Strikes a quarrel tho' no Blood appear
Who weares a Hatt or Spurr, o'erturns a Bell
Or by unfkillful handling fpoils a Peal
Shall fixpence pay for every fingle crime
I will make him careful againft another time.

Let's all in love and friendfhip hither come
Whilft the fhrill Treble calls to Thondring tom,
And fince Bells are for modeft Recreation:
Let's rife and Ring and fall to Admiration:

Ringers' rules, St Endellion, c 1735

twelve penny loaves should be distributed to twelve poor parishioners after evening service on Sundays!

In 1756 and 1761 the old churches at Redruth and Helston were taken down and new classical-style buildings erected in their place. Helston church had long been semi-ruinous as the result of a violent storm. At Redruth the late fifteenth- or early sixteenth-century tower was retained, and the threefold roof construction was repeated in the new church, but in both cases a large auditorium with no formal chancel was achieved within. At Redruth two lines of Tuscan columns divide the interior. These room-like structures prompted the comment that they resembled rather 'a gymnasium for training cavalry than a place of religious worship'.

It was the Age of Reason, and rationalism desired the end of mystery. In several places remaining stained windows were taken out, as at St Mary's, Truro, in the 1740s, and plain wooden framed clear glass substitutes put in their place. At Paul one or two such still exist. Screens, too, fell into disfavour. The old screen at Madron was removed to facilitate performance of one of Handel's Oratorios in 1751!

Akin to this 'rationalism' was the fashion of 'Grecianising' or 'Italianising' the medieval interiors by loading the pillars and arcades with plaster worked into classical mouldings. St Gluvias and St Mary's, Truro, were treated in this way, and prints of the latter church can still be seen although the actual classicising has long since been removed.

In the mid-eighteenth century a new interest in the vocal accompaniment of the services led to the gathering of better-trained choirs and the expenses of new books, treats and instruments such as bass viols, bassoons, violins and so forth. A few relics remain from this time, such as old psalm books and a violoncello from St Ervan. But the damp of Cornwall does not contribute towards survival. In some places the singing was led by barrel organs (not to be confused with street pianos, once incorrectly so-called). There were sufficient instruments of this sort by the end of the century for William Wills, a clockmaker from Truro, to advertise his skill in repairing and restoring them. All have now vanished from the Cornish churches, though the barrels remain at Probus.

Inlaid pulpits at St Mary's, Truro, and St Levan, as well as other fine pieces of furniture elsewhere, testify to the continuing enrichment of the churches. So too, in another way, does the large-scale provision of sundials in the later eighteenth

century. Many of these, as at St Buryan, 1747, St Enoder, 1766, North Hill, 1753, Sancreed, 1762, display considerable skill in the calculation of the dials as well as in the engraving, on the slate of which most are constructed.

The end of the eighteenth century, however, and the opening years of the nineteenth show the Cornish church reaching its lowest point, both in the activity of the parishes and the state of the buildings. Repair and maintenance was traditionally financed by a church rate levied on the parishioners at the annual church vestry. A growing resistance to the payment of this levy and a grudging of money

Font and cover, Falmouth, 1759

spent on the buildings led to a running down in their condition and to the execution of repair work in the cheapest and shoddiest style.

The rural deans' notebooks report conditions first hand as the churches were inspected, and they contain some sorry evidence. At Crowan in 1808 the clock was out of order, the organ broken down, and the church needed whitewashing and a new chancel door. At St Enoder in 1820 the floor was still earth, though well-sanded, and the roof was not ceiled. Whitstone had ivy growing within the church. The walls of St

Breward chancel were 'miserably green and damp'. In 1821 the rural dean found the font at Lanteglos-by-Camelford painted blue, as was the pulpit at Michaelstowe in 1818. The sand at St Endoc had reached and even covered the roof on the northeast side in the same year. The many minor deficiencies in the books and furniture all too eloquently told of a reduced interest and slovenly care of the churches. The replies to the bishops' Visitation Queries of this period show plainly the fall in attendances compared with the mid-eighteenth century.

The prevailing understanding of church usage and architecture is reflected in the buildings erected or remodelled in the first thirty years of the nineteenth century. St Michael's, Penwerris (1827) is a square room with a gallery at one end. Its attempts at 'gothick' flavour are three pepper pot castellated turrets on the front. The church at Morvah was remodelled in 1828 as one square room, the old arcades being discarded and all original features except the tower destroyed. St Day church, erected in 1828 to serve the great mining population of that area, was a high galleried spacious block, with two rows of windows and a pinnacled turret with battlements in a Commissioner's gothick mode. Within, its slender piers and high ceilings produced an effect far removed from that of medieval buildings; it could seat twelve hundred people. About the same time St Erme was remodelled (1820). Here the arcades were retained, but set wider apart and something of the old preserved, though on the outside one roof ornamented with pinnacles covers the whole. St John's, Truro (1827) makes no pretensions to gothickry, but is in the Italianate style.

St Mary's, Penzance, built 1836 to the design of Charles Hutchins on the site of a spired medieval chapel by then too small for the population, is a stately achievement. Its galleried spaciousness is more satisfying than that of St Day, and the more modern adaptions to contemporary usage enhance its dignity, of which the fine site is part. From some way away one may be pardoned for thinking it a grand medieval church, until a closer examination discloses the galleried interior which once seated two thousand.

The energetic episcopate of Henry Phillpotts, bishop of Exeter 1831–69, coincided with the first years of the Oxford Movement and the accompanying Church revival which set men again to study the principles of Church doctrine and practice and the design of the buildings in which they were declared. The Ecclesiological Society, developing out of the Cambridge Camden Society in the 1840s, gave wide publicity through its periodicals to the styles and features of church architecture of different periods. Many of its judgements were precious and stilted, but the enthusiasm enkindled for old churches issued in a tremendous though ill-informed series of efforts at restoration.

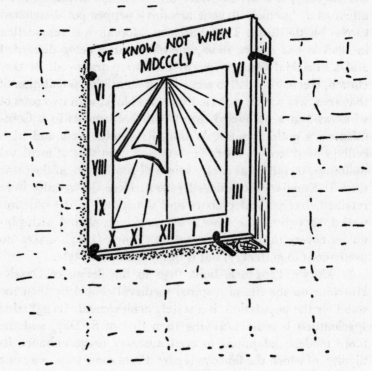

Sundial at St Wenn, 1855

Phillpotts found his diocese underchurched. New communities had sprung up around prosperous mines, and often the parish church was miles away from the new town. Various nonconformist groups had erected their places of worship, and the Anglican authorities were awakened to act. In Phillpotts' time some thirty-six new churches were built to serve new parishes or districts. Many of these buildings, such as Mount Hawke, Carnmenellis or Lanner, possess little architectural merit, but time has mellowed them and their dignified furnishing given them an atmosphere. Some incorporate ancient features brought from elsewhere, for instance, the ancient fonts at Tideford, Washaway and Herodsfoot and formerly at Carnmenellis. At Pendeen, in a thriving mining community, the vigorous and evangelical vicar Robert Aitken got the miners together to build a new church to his own design (1851), which he professed was based on the abbey at Iona.

The effect of the study of architecture at this time can be clearly seen by comparing such churches as Baldhu (1848) or St George's, Truro (1855)—both from the designs of an earnest ecclesiologist, Rev William Haslam, vicar of Baldhu—with such an erection as the church at Penwerris. Stiff and artificial as the details are, they reveal a clearer understanding of the proportions and function of ancient places of worship which they desired to copy.

One lasting mistake the ecclesiologists of the time made was to modify the parish churches on cathedral lines. Chancels were filled with stalls and robed choirs; organs swelled to fill transepts or chancel aisles, and the old church bands were dismissed summarily. Only in recent years has the mistake been realised and the chancel once again cleared to allow the altar to stand in simple dignity, perhaps still behind its screen or possibly now before it, but in something like the proportion for which the church originally found its shape.

The peak of the high Victorian gothic is of course to be found in the cathedral at Truro, of which J. L. Pearson was the architect. The bishopric of Truro was founded in 1876 and the

47

new bishop, Edward White Benson, enthroned in 1877 in the old parish church of St Mary's, Truro. This church was soon seen to be far too small for a cathedral and the new building was commenced in 1880, part of the old church—the south aisle—being incorporated as an extra choir aisle giving a fine series of those vistas for which Pearson had a liking. The construction occupied thirty years, the western towers being built last, and the cathedral was dedicated in 1910. So full of fascinating detail is the building, and so remarkable a witness to the Victorian upsurge of enthusiasm is its completion and furnishing, that those interested are directed to the illustrated guides available in the cathedral and elsewhere.

With the erection of new churches, some—such as J. D. Sedding's St Elwyn, Hayle (1886) and All Saints', Falmouth (1887)—of considerable merit, went the restoration of the majority of the churches of Cornwall. The abolition of the church rate in 1868 left the care of the fabric of the parish church to the sense of responsibility of the parishioners. In fact for a time there was released much private generosity and initiative over which the vestry had little control. Enthusiastic clergy or beneficent squires could restore and remodel the churches out of their own pockets and many did so, no doubt much to the dismay of the locals. The faculty law seems at this time to have concerned itself only with the main structure.

At Quethiock the roof was partly off when Rev William Willimott went there in 1878. He set to work to restore the church, and the story is an epic in itself. With his own hands he carved panels, altar fronts and chairs, made stained windows of some merit, and painted screens. Rev Clement Winstanley Carlyon of St Just-in-Roseland made new seats and pulpit for St Anthony-in-Roseland in 1851, and supervised the restoration of the building himself. In addition to such amateur architects, there were the professionals, including William White, who designed the church at Mithian (1861) and restored many others; George Street, who so admired the spire and lantern at Lostwithiel that he made it the basis of his design for his first

Page 49 *St Piran's Oratory, sixth to seventh century. The brick supports and the protecting building are modern*

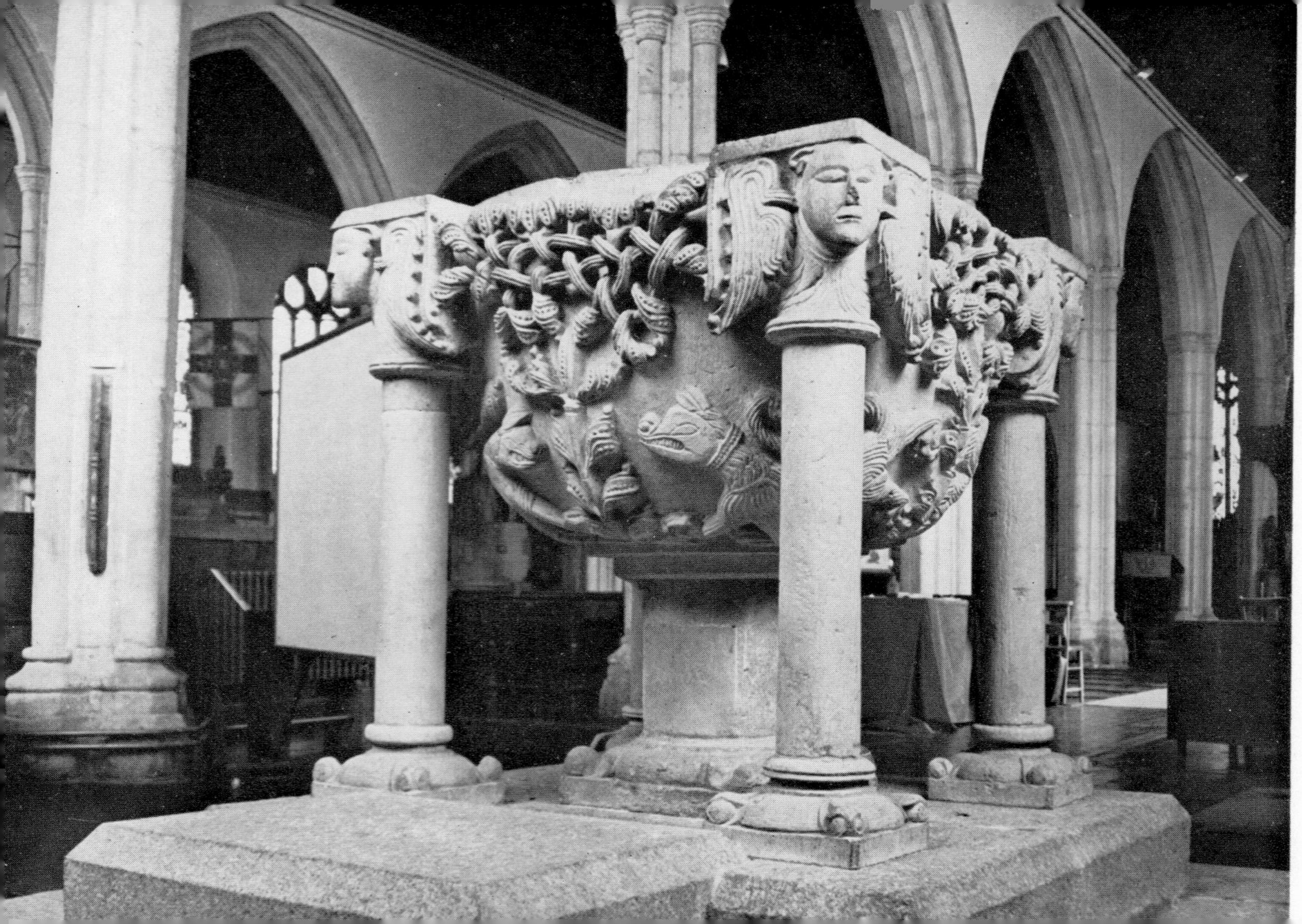

 Norman font, Bodmin

complete church at Biscovey (1849); Thomas Hardy, who restored St Juliot (1872) and married the rector's sister-in-law; J. D. Sedding, already mentioned, a man of sympathy for old work, who enlarged St Paul's, Truro (1883). A relation of his, Edmund Sedding, also restored with conserving zeal and carried out research into the Norman architecture of the county.

A member of the St Aubyn family, J. Piers St Aubyn, was an energetic and widely employed restorer of churches between 1845 and 1885; his work usually left little behind to remind us of ancient days. Pitchpine, shiny tiles, new openwork in ceilings, crested ridge tiles, iron gable crosses and bootscrapers at the porch door will be easily recognised as his trademark. No doubt the condition of many churches demanded preservation skills beyond those available, but one cannot enter an over-restored church without a pang for what could have been saved.

Marble, mosaic and coloured reredoses, painted texts on walls and elaborate embroidery may still be found in profusion in numbers of Cornish churches, and, with a new appreciation of Victorian ecclesiastical art, these may well become valued again. Generations immediately past have preferred to hide and forget them in many cases!

Not a few churches, such as Blisland, Crantock, Tintagel, St Buryan, St Columb Major, Poundstock and St Endellion, have been carefully handled and restored to recover something of the medieval spirit and produce a sense of mystery and drama as a helpful setting for worship.

By the dawn of the twentieth century there was an accumulating body of studies of Cornish architecture and a new readiness to treat sympathetically what remained from ancient days. Architects of the present day are not likely to repeat the heavy-handed treatment of the churches common a century ago. Nevertheless, all too frequently new furnishings are bought from mass-producing shops with little regard for local material or tradition.

Several modern churches of true Cornish flavour have been erected. St Michael's, Newquay (1911) is built in native style

Victorian brass, Lanlivery, c 1880

with local materials, and the interior is light and dignified by
modern screenwork and a magnificent new organ with case in
the eighteenth-century fashion. The new tower, however,
though grand, is somewhat un-Cornish. At Carbis Bay, St Ives,
a patient and consistent campaign of building piecemeal to a
thoroughly Cornish and pleasing plan was completed in 1968
with the erection of the last part of the nave. Weathered native
stone from the local mine buildings and the pinnacles from the

tower at Pendeen help to give a truly Cornish appearance to this church.

The town of Camelford, long without an Anglican place of worship, was furnished between the wars with a small church in local stone which is interestingly planned. At Wadebridge, Penwerris and Trevone, near Padstow, daughter churches of modern lines can be seen.

The abandonment of the old church at St Day owing to its dangerously deteriorated stonework led to the completion of a well-planned church centre (1967) in contemporary style, which has been highly praised by modern architectural authorities as one of the most significant church buildings in the south-west.

A good deal of recent informed improvement has also been carried out. A Georgian preaching box church at Torpoint was transformed in the 1930s under the direction of Sir Charles Nicholson into a place full of dignity and atmosphere. Charles-town possesses the first re-ordering in the diocese with a central altar in front of the screen, the chancel doing duty as a Lady chapel. This work was done under the supervision of S. Dykes Bower, an architect of distinction, and witnesses to the contemporary desire to place emphasis on sharing congregationally in the altar service. Other churches, as at St Paul's, Truro, and Helston, have been prompted to follow this fashion.

The increasing cost of careful repairs and the lengthening age of the buildings place great responsibility on incumbents and church councils. The Inspection of Churches Measure now ensures that every five years a qualified architect makes a detailed inspection and report on necessary repairs and restora-tions. This enactment has done a great deal to bring the churches into fair condition, as deterioration can be checked before it becomes irremediable. Parishes, however, are still left with the responsibility of raising the greater part of the funds and carrying out the work. How far the congregations should continue to be liable for the upkeep of what are increasingly recognised as national treasures can be debated.

The faculty jurisdiction now ensures that any significant work planned is submitted to a diocesan advisory committee before innovations or alterations are permitted by the diocesan chancellor. Incumbents can also obtain helpful advice from the experts who serve on such committees, and from the central Places of Worship Commission, a body in touch with acknowledged authorities in the different spheres of ecclesiastical art and architecture.

As a result of this concern visitors will find most churches in the county—as elsewhere—well cared for and usually furnished with guide books and so forth, the fruit of careful research and study of the heritage of our ancient shrines.

It will be appreciated that the churches are the property of the parishioners, and are not merely museums of ancient or beautiful things. They are still the centres of living worship. The buildings and their contents derive their meaning from, and are only fully understood within, the context of the local community engaged in the worship of Almighty God.

It is hoped that these introductory chapters, together with the notes on each church in the following pages, will be found to stimulate an interest and help the enquiring visitor to know what to look for in Cornish churches.

Cornish Churches
An Alphabetical List

It will be understood from the introductory chapters that in many instances there was a Celtic oratory or place of worship on the site of the present church. Of these, nothing remains which can be identified with certainty, except some ancient crosses and the oratories at Perranporth and Gwithian. But the fact, attested by the place names, that a great number of the parish churches possess a Celtic origin, adds interest to the sites so long used for Christian worship.

The alterations, restorations and repairs in different periods and styles have left many problems of interpretation and dating. Without lengthy and detailed explanations a complete picture of the stages by which any church attained its present form cannot be given. All that is attempted in the following notes is a general dating of the main parts of each building. The interested reader is invited to refer to the many books which deal exclusively with the architecture of the Cornish churches in great detail.

The list of other things to NOTE does not pretend to be exhaustive. Individuals will find interest in almost everything within and without our churches, and guide books will describe in fuller fashion the various features of the church to which they refer. Here, however, the enquirer will find a handy list with which to begin his exploration and the mention of things which might otherwise be overlooked. Common features such as organs and rings of bells are noted only where there is some unusual interest.

The presence of daughter churches or chapels-of-ease, many

of them Victorian, is a characteristic of the Cornish scene. Many are somewhat featureless, erected to fulfil a purpose and without much attention to architectural grace. Some, however, are ancient, as those in the parishes of St Minver and St Winnow. These chapels-of-ease are mentioned in the following list only where there is some antiquity or ground for general interest.

Similarly, the churches of other denominations, some of architectural merit or with a touching story of homespun devotion, really require a separate treatment and therefore do not find mention in these pages.

In the following list the names of the parishes appear in alphabetical order, disregarding the prefix 'St'. Thus, St Erney will be found under 'E'. The whole name as it occurs will be listed under the appropriate letter—for example, North Petherwin is under N and not P. The letter 'D' preceding each entry indicates the dedication of the church.

ADVENT   D. St Athwenna
Present church—chancel, nave, south aisle, north transept, porch chiefly 15th cent, west tower 14th cent. Restored 1847–8.
NOTE: Norman font; south transept closed, after collapse of roof in snowstorm about 1870; flamboyant east window, one of few in county; odd steps inside up to tower; north transept part of 13th cent church; porch doorway of catacleuse stone; remote situation; local effort at restoration after threat of closure.

Guide

ST AGNES   D. St Agnes
Present church—chancel, nave, north and south aisles, porch with covered way to separate choir vestry, west tower with spire. Until 1846 a chapelry in Perranzabuloe. Rebuilt in 1848 by J. P. St Aubyn, except tower. At reflooring in 1931 bases of piers of 1482 church were revealed, and traces of foundations of

earlier structures 12ft by 18ft, probably a pre-Norman chapel.
NOTE: Font, possibly in catacleuse stone; curious Elizabethan
wooden almsbox in form of a hungry man; stonework of high
altar from old quay at St Agnes; tablets to members of Tonkin
family and to mine captain who died in Rio de Janiero 1850;
stations of the cross by Lang family of Oberammergau; steeply
sloping site.

ST ALLEN   D. St Alunus

Present church—chancel, nave, south aisle of 15th cent, porch
and tower of three stages at west end, with turret and spirelet.
Probably a Norman church stood here. Lancet in north chancel
wall and blocked north door to nave, possibly 13th cent.
NOTE: Stem and base of font probably Norman, bowl perhaps
a cross base; Royal Arms 1660; medieval bell in tower; old
communion rails round font; piscina and traces of 13th cent
arch in chancel; corbel head, east end south aisle; carved
reading desk dated 1618; slate memorial John Marten 1626;
fine Celtic cross in churchyard. A former incumbent was Sir
Harry Trelawny, an eccentric who became a Presbyterian
minister at Looe in 1777, was ordained a priest in the Church of
England 1781 and became a Roman Catholic in 1810, being
ordained a Roman Catholic priest in 1830.

ALTARNUN   D. St Nonna

Present church—chancel, nave, north and south aisles; porches
and lofty west tower of three stages. Norman church stood here.
Spacious and wide. Chiefly 15th and 16th cent. Restored 1867.
Much old woodwork remains in roofs, screens, notable bench
ends, communion rails.
NOTE: Grand Norman font; fragment of Norman capital in
vestry wall; Norman piscina bowl and shaft; communion rails
dated 1684; notable screen; 79 splendid bench ends, notably
jester, fiddler, etc; paintings c 1610 in chancel; custom here of
officiant at Holy Communion standing behind altar, of very
long continuance; tomb in churchyard of Digory and Elizabeth

ST ANTHONY-IN-MENEAGE

Isbell 1795, who in 1743 entertained the Wesleys on their first visits to Cornwall; slate memorial carved with a nail by Nevill Northey Burnard, later a famous sculptor, at age 14. This is the largest parish in extent in Cornwall: 15,018 acres.

Guide

ST ANTHONY-IN-MENEAGE
D. St Antoninus
(possibly assimilated from a Celtic name)

Present church—12th cent nave, chancel and south transept; 15th cent north aisle and west tower. Restored carefully in 1890. Some old woodwork remains, and modern enrichment. NOTE: Font, 15th cent, similar to St Winnow; broken base of 12th cent font; old roofs with carved bosses; 13th cent stoup in porch; dog door in tower door; angel figures supporting pinnacles on tower; organ 1954; 18 fine brass chandeliers and wall sconces; medieval bell c 1500; roodloft stairs, door on outside.

Guide

ST ANTHONY-IN-ROSELAND
D. St Antoninus

Present church—cruciform church re-dedicated 1259, with a small establishment settled by Plympton Priory. Norman doorway probably a throw-out from Plympton, then rebuilding. Central tower arches are 13th cent. At the Dissolution the people claimed the nave; the chancel was pulled down by the lay proprietor to whom the monastic property was given. The church thus had the form of a T. Hence the local verse:

St Anthony church in the form of a T
The parson doth preach in the belfree.

Restoration in 1850s and much rebuilding; design and some carving by amateur architect, Rev Clement Winstanley Carlyon, rector of St Just.
NOTE: Norman doorway, with off-centre Agnes Dei; belfry

58

arches; piscinas; carved woodwork of 19th cent; memorial tablets to Spry and other families of Place; entrance to house, once monastic buildings; stone coffin in churchyard.

Guide

ANTONY D. St James

Present church—chancel, nave, north and south aisles, porches and west tower. Rededicated 1259, and some traces of 13th cent work exist. Mostly, however, 15th cent.

NOTE: Brass of Margery Arundell, 1420 (ask permission to rub); Carew family memorials, including Richard Carew, author of the *Survey of Cornwall*; Lady altar an ancient chest; sedilia, piscinas; niche in east window, north aisle; painted spandrels in arcades; some traces of ancient glass; figure of Virgin in Lady chapel belonged to Queen Alexandra; windows by Kempe 1888 and Clayton & Bell 1860; stocks; one-handed clock in tower; cresset stone; war memorial to nearby naval establishments; splendid view from steep steps to church, which Turner is said to have admired. Included in this parish is:

Maryfield (D. SS Philip and James) was once an estate church for Antony House.

Present church—chancel, nave, north aisle, south transept, west tower and spire. Erected 1865 by William White. Now (1972) a district church.

NOTE: Marble colums; red and white stone arches; good tracery; one continental well-cast bell with heads on canons (inaccessible).

ST AUSTELL D. St Austol

Present church—chancel with aisles, nave, north and south aisles, porches (south one with parvise) and west tower of late 15th cent, three stages, many statues and panels. Norman church with choir aisles, and a chantry alongside, involved in an ambitious 15th cent nave reconstruction. Restored and enriched.

NOTE: Grand Norman font; columns and arches in Lady chapel of Norman date; parvise over porch; outstanding statues, heraldic panels and emblems of the passion on tower; medieval bench ends in tower; good modern woodwork in nave seating; tablets to local families, including Samuel Drew, shoemaker metaphysician; memorial windows, one to Bishop Colenso, controversial figure in Victorian biblical criticism; twenty-four-hour clock dial on west face of tower.

Guide

BALDHU D. St Michael

Present church—chancel, nave, south aisle, porch, tower and spire on north side. Built 1848 from design of Rev William Haslam, then perpetual curate of this parish. Possibly erected to meet the needs of a mining population.
NOTE: Ecclesiological Society style detail in stonework; chandeliers; modern statues; tomb in churchyard of Billy Bray, Cornish revivalist preacher, 1794–1868.

ST BLAZEY D. St Blaise

Present church—chancel, nave, north and south aisles, porch and west tower. Wholly 15th cent construction c 1440. There was originally a right of way through the tower from north to south. Early in 19th cent the west end of north aisle was lengthened and cut it off. Restored 1839 and 1897.
NOTE: Niche for statue on tower; great granite slabs in walls; slate memorial to 17th cent merchant; monument to Henry Scobell, treasurer to Queen Anne; good modern windows; clock in tower in memory of former vicar, Rev George Polgrean 1971 who ministered here for over 30 years and has a street named after him, a unique tribute.

BLISLAND D. SS Protus and Hyacinth

Present church—chancel, nave, north chapel, south aisle, transepts, porch and tower of three stages with stair turret (16th cent) at north of north transept. Traces of all styles of architecture from Norman to 15th cent. Ornamented screen and interior and careful restoration largely the result of interest of Rev Vernon Edward-Collins, Tractarian squire-parson of Victorian days, himself a skilled artist and embroiderer. Much later enrichment.

NOTE: Two fonts, one Norman, one 15th cent; traces of Norman door on north nave wall; peculiar fleur-de-lys tracery in window of north nave wall; roofs showing settlement and buttressed piers; noteworthy brass to John Balsam, rector, 1410 (ask permission to rub); slate memorial with effigy Humfry Kempe 1624 and Susanna Toker 1686; Royal Arms James I 1604; screen; delicately carved fruit on pulpit; south transept remodelled 18th cent as Lavethan pew; good modern memorial tablets; old crosses in churchyard; 'Grecian' remains below churchyard recall leisured days of Regency parsons and summer houses.

Guide

BOCONNOC   D. Unknown
Present church—chancel, nave, south aisle, short north aisle or family pew; porch and gable bell turret. Chiefly 15th cent. Restored 1873.
NOTE: Font 15th cent; Jacobean altar made by Raynold Mohun in 1621; Jacobean pulpit; old chairs in family pew; musicians' gallery; north transept screen, part of Bradoc roodscreen; King Charles I occupied this pew in August 1644 while conducting the Civil War campaign around Lostwithiel; 19th cent memorial windows; wall monument with punning epitaph to Will Drew's widow 1637; stone monument with Time and Death 16th cent.

Guide

BODMIN   D. St Petroc
Present church—chancel, nave, north and south aisles, parvise

porch with two stories, tower (Norman base) on north side, walls 8ft thick. Largest church in Cornwall. Sole ancient survival in town which had many ecclesiastical establishments including a priory, friary, and continuous monastic life from time of St Petroc. Norman and probably originally cruciform, but now 15th cent. Spire on this tower struck by lightning 1699. Norman doorway at west end no longer exists, and Norman capitals remain in neighbourhood. Chancel arch over nave and aisles is unusual in Cornwall. Carefully restored at various times and enriched. Old woodwork in pulpit, division between chancel and south chapel, etc.

NOTE: Grand Norman font, best of its kind in the county; 12th cent reliquary of St Petroc, in which his bones were returned after having been stolen in 1177; pillar piscina and others; south porch with groined roof; pulpit; icon presented by Russian Language School; organ, in part 1775; tomb of Prior Vyvyan, titular bishop of Megara, in catacleuse stone, 1533; a few carved bench ends—the contract with Matthy More who carved the woodwork still exists, signed in 1491; colours of many regiments stationed here; chantry of St Thomas of Canterbury, ruin at east end, long used as a school; pillar of old friary in churchyard; St Guron's well; pinnacles of old tower; slate memorial with effigy Peter Bolt 1633; Jowdy, Katheren and Richard Durant 1589, 1608, 1632; curfew rung daily at 8pm—this curfew mentioned by John Wesley in Journal, Monday 29 August 1743: being on trackless Bodmin moor, had 'got quite out of the way; but we had not gone far before we heard Bodmin bell'.

BOLVENTOR   D. Holy Trinity

Present church—cruciform, vestry (once chancel), nave, transepts, porch, central turret over crossing. Erected 1848. Re-ordered in 1965, a simple moorland sanctuary, with central altar and former chancel used as vestry. A medieval chapel of St Luke once existed nearby. The font is now at Tideford.

NOTE: Central stone altar; modern crucifix with Christ robed as high priest.

Guide

BOTUS FLEMING   D. St Mary

Present church—chancel, nave, north aisle, porch and west tower of three stages. Mostly 15th cent. Rededicated 1259, but added to by erection of north aisle and tower. Drastic restoration 1872.

NOTE: Effigy in niche, a Valletort (?); pillars with Breton-like niches and canopies for statues; piscina; roodloft stairs; sundial 1787; stocks; rough-cast tower; Plymouth limestone south wall, brought up river creek which once flowed near churchyard; good 18th cent Wall tablets, including Michael Loam, born here, who invented the man-engine which relieved miners of long ladder climbs; ancient holy well with figure of Virgin in niche (50yd from east gateway).

BOYTON   D. The Holy Name

Present church—chancel, nave, south aisle 15th cent; porch, west tower of three stages 14th cent; early Norman, or perhaps Saxon, font shows a church of that date stood here. Enlarged in the 14th and 15th cents. Restored 1876–7. Some old woodwork survives.

NOTE: Font, possibly Saxon; some part of chancel screen; old roofs; 18th cent organ case; fragments of old glass; piscina in chancel; coat of arms; tablet to benefactor William Symonds 1662; stained windows.

BRADOC   D. St Mary

Present church—chancel, nave, south aisle, north transept or chapel, porch and west tower. Norman cruciform church? Now mostly 13th cent. Some interesting old woodwork remains in bench ends, screen base, panels and roof.

NOTE: Norman font; carved panels to pew fronts; base of screen (part taken to Boconnoc); Elizabethan pulpit; alabaster reredos;

heraldic glass in windows; old chest carved and painted; odd arches and pier to north transept—19th cent reconstruction (?); one pinnacle on tower perhaps from chapel of St Nectan in St Winnow.

Guide

BREAGE D. St Breaca

Present church—chancel, nave, north and south aisles, north and south transepts, porch and three-stage west tower, all 15th cent. Restored 1890-1. Some old woodwork remains.

NOTE: Roman milestone in church; wall paintings of St Christopher and Christ of the Trades; memorial to Margaret Godolphin 1678; helmets with Godolphin crest; memorial windows; 19th cent reredos carved by Belgian craftsmen; modern screen; sundial 1795; cross head in churchyard.

Guide

ST BREOKE D. St Briocus

Present church—long chancel, nave, north and south transepts, south aisle, porches, tower at west end. Still traces of 13th cent as dedicated by Bishop Bronescombe in 1259, except south aisle late 14th cent, remodelled late 15th cent. No old woodwork except in porches. Restored 1881.

NOTE: 15th cent catacleuse font; parts of ancient brasses 1520-30 (ask permission to rub); reredos in alabaster 1908; large and imposing slate memorials with effigies and heraldic details to William and Jane Vyell 1598, Charles Tredeneck 1578; others of 17th cent to members of Tregagle family; 13th cent coffin lid; 19th cent slate tablets of commandments and creed; Royal Arms Queen Anne 1710; old chest; chandelier, foreign and modern but noteworthy; record mark of height (4ft 9in) of floodwater in church 1965.

Hall church of St Mary built 1951 in Wadebridge with good modern ornaments and arrangements.

Guide

ST BREWARD   D. St Brueredus

Present church—chancel, nave, north and south aisles, north transept and chapel, porch and west tower of three stages 15th cent. Norman church, possibly cruciform. Restored 1864 by J. P. St Aubyn. Some old woodwork in south aisle, roof, bench ends and screen to Hengar pew.

NOTE: Odd-shaped font—Norman cut down (?); three piers of Norman north arcade reconstructed; lancet window in wall near tower; piscina in south aisle wall; slate memorials with effigies Lewis Adams 1609, Christopher Rogers 1609, Nicholas Burrough 1654, William Billing 1654; old photographs of worked stone details in parish, including one of arch once in chapel on Roughtor; woodwork to Hengar pew; stone cat's head on outside of tower; two stone heads by door; courses of large and small granite stones in tower; sundial 1792; Royal Arms William III 1700.

BUDE HAVEN   D. St Michael

Present church—chancel, nave, transepts, north porch, baptistry and vestry. George Wightwick architect. Built 1835, with enlargements.

NOTE: Good 19th cent windows; shrine of Our Lady of Walsingham; striking modern statue of St Michael; memorials; figurehead memorial in parish hall to men shipwrecked in the *Bencoolen* in 1862.

BUDOCK   D. St Budocus

Present church—chancel, nave, south transept, north aisle, porch and three-stage west tower. Mostly 15th cent enlargement of 13th cent church, whose lancet windows remain in · chancel and transept.

NOTE: Replica of reliquary of St Budock in niche over porch door; roodscreen restored, but paintings visible in panels of older part; brass to John Killigrew 1567 (ask permission to rub); low box pews; piscinas; panelled jambs to porch doorway; memorial windows; slate-hung church room in churchyard.

Guide

ST BURYAN   D. St Beriana

Present church—chancel, nave, north and south aisles, porch and four-stage tower at west end. Traditionally founded by King Athelstan. Collegiate church in 13th cent, on Norman foundations. Mostly now 15th cent. Drastic restoration 1814 and 1874, much careful rehabilitation since. Some old woodwork in screen, stalls, etc.

NOTE: Norman-style arches in north chancel wall; old collegiate return stalls; restored screen with good old carving; 13th cent coffin lid in church; modern tower screen and other memorials; sundial; 15th cent font; crosses and coped stone in churchyard; one of the four bells has flaw caused by man jumping off hedge near the mould before the metal was set; curious headstone in churchyard to William Simpson Doble.

CALLINGTON   D. St Mary

Present church—chancel, nave, south aisle and double north aisle, the second one by J. D. Sedding 1882, porch and three-stage noble west tower. Clerestory in nave, a rare feature in Cornwall. Surviving Norman font shows a chapelry existed here before the present fine 15th cent church. Restored 1858 by J. P. St Aubyn, enriched in later times. The tower and bells burnt out in 1895.

NOTE: Fine Norman font; old altar in south chapel; clerestory; fine brass to Nicholas Aysshton, benefactor of this church and a judge of some eminence 1466 (ask permission to rub); alabaster effigy of first Lord Willoughby de Broke 1502 (regrettably vandalised by initial cutting), with figures of monks with rosaries at feet; lantern cross; slate memorial Ann Holliday 1753 (porch wall, outside); angel corbels support the tower pinnacles; buttresses between nave windows.

Guide

Page 67 *West Front,*
St Germans,
twelfth century

Page 68 *Chancel detail, St Ive, fourteenth century*

CALSTOCK   D. St Andrew

Present church—chancel, nave, north and south aisles, porch and west tower of three stages. Arcades 13th and 14th cents, tower and porch 15th cent. Vestry at east end of north aisle once a private mortuary, added 1588, 17th cent monuments to the Edgecumbe family. Another vestry, 19th cent, on south side. Restored 1886–7. Old woodwork in roofs.

NOTE: Large porch and granite memorial in floor; aperture near floor in porch, a fireplace, probably the only one in Cornwall; faint remains of wall painting on north arcade spandrels; roodloft stairs; roofs; ringers' rules and picture c 1775; niche over east window; Royal Arms George III 1816; stoup; memorials in churchyard to miners killed in accidents; view from churchyard.

Gunnislake (D. St Anne), is one of several 19th cent chapels-of-ease in this extensive parish. It is striking, with the floor descending in steps to the chancel, and granite piers without capitals.

CAMBORNE D. SS Meriadocus and Martin

Present church—chancel, nave, north aisle and double south aisle, the outer one by J. P. St Aubyn 1878; porch and west tower. Mostly 15th cent. Restored 1862. A few scraps of old woodwork in porch roof, bench ends and pulpit.

NOTE: Ancient altar slab, probably Saxon; marble altar piece 1761; roodloft stairs; bench ends; chandelier; Pendarves monuments; chair carved by lady parishioner; piscina; stoup; panels on pulpit; ancient cross in churchyard.

CARBIS BAY D. St Anta and All Saints

Present church—chancel, nave, south aisle, west and south porches, organ transept and tower at southeast of three stages. A wooden mission church was erected here in 1913. The foundation of the present church was laid 1927, and the first part, chancel, one bay of nave and part of tower, was dedicated

E

1929. Tower finished 1959. Nave completed 1964–8, when the whole church was consecrated. It is wholly in a Cornish traditional style, except the upper stage of the tower, which has no belfry lights. The sound of ten bells—the only ring of that number in Cornwall apart from the Cathedral—escapes via a lantern on the tower roof. Architect R. F. Wheatly of Truro. Weathered local stone was obtained from old mine buildings donated for the purpose.

NOTE: Granite altars; five-light east window of chancel and south window of Lady chapel; stained windows with Cornish themes; pulpit; lectern; old font from Lelant, the mother parish; modern carved woodwork; Italian crucifix; children's corner; tower details; circular window at west end of nave; ring of ten bells.

Guide

CARDINHAM   D. St Meubred

Present church—chancel, nave, north and south aisles, porch and stately west three-stage tower, all mostly 15th cent. The great medieval family of the Dinhams lived here. The church is spacious and magnificent for a moorland parish. Much excellent old woodwork in roofs of aisles, bench ends, seats, etc. NOTE: Norman font, once lost and replaced by Georgian substitute (still extant) refixed in old place; brass to Thomas Awmarle, rector 1401 (ask permission to rub); elaborate monument to William Glynn 1699; Easter sepulchre in north sanctuary wall; sepulchral slab; niche and corbel from earlier church; 71 bench ends; good modern stained glass; stocks; sedilia with inscribed stones from previous use; belfry screen, perhaps gallery front or classical reredos; Royal Arms Charles II 1661; old sideboard displays panels of Coronation of the Virgin; sundial 1739; large and notable old cross in churchyard.

CARNMENELLIS   D. Holy Trinity

A Victorian church with lofty chancel and nave and bell

turret on gable was erected 1850 to serve a once-thriving
mining community. First priest was Rev William Broadley
who, with his wife, was earnestly evangelical with Tractarian
sympathies. The widowed Mrs Broadley became a member and
later Superior of the London Community of the Holy Name
(still in existence). Later she retired to Carnmenellis, being
known as 'Mother Maria Charlotte'. This church was her care
and spiritual centre. After many vicissitudes the church was
left destitute of population, became ruinous and was demolished
1970. The Broadley tomb is preserved.

CHACEWATER   D. St Paul
Present church—chancel, nave, north and south aisles, porch
and west tower. Originally built 1828, and remodelled 1892 to
design of Edmund Sedding, except tower. Nave has a clerestory
and granite and Polyphant arcades.
NOTE: Clerestoried nave; sanctuary; pulpit in memory of
Bishop Wilkinson 1883–91; stained east window once in St
Mary's, Truro; lectern; lychgate.

CHARLESTOWN   D. St Paul
Present church—chancel, nave, lean-to north and south aisles,
transepts, porch and tower at west end of north aisle by
Christopher Eales. Consecrated 1851. Spire added (fibreglass
on completed tower) 1971. Reordering with altar under crossing by S. Dykes Bower.
NOTE: Central altar—first such in the diocese; spire; belfry
screen; peal of six bells 1972 by Taylor of Loughborough.

ST CLEER   D. St Clarus
Present church—chancel, nave, north and south aisles, porch
and west tower of three stages, of stately proportion. Norman
font bowl and other survivals show a church of that period
stood here. Now mostly 15th cent but Norman work in reconstructed piers of north arcade and north door, rebuilt when

south aisle added. All heavily restored 1877, but softened with later enrichments.

NOTE: Norman font, door and possibly stonework in arcade; Polyphant south arcade; piscina in chancel; another with squint in north aisle; memorials and windows; modern screen 1904; slate memorial to Robert Langford, with curious 'creed' of Langford charity, 1614; painted wood panels (1662) in spandrels of arcades; Victorian pulpit; Royal Arms 1708; pewter tankard 17th cent. Holy well near church.

Guide

ST CLEMENT   D. St Clement

Present church—chancel, nave, north transept, south aisle 15th cent, porch and west tower of three stages. Only the tower base and the lower part of the north wall of nave recall the 13th cent church. Drastic restoration in 1860s. Only a few fragments of old woodwork. Modern reordering in 1960s.

NOTE: Almsbox dated 1728; memorial on south wall; pieces of old roof timbers in belfry and chapel screens; ancient inscribed stone in churchyard 4th cent (?); slate headstone to a servant who asked for her wages to be reduced as age made her less able to do her work; stocks; church house or lychgate with room over.

ST CLETHER   D. St Clederus

Present church—chancel, nave, south aisle, porch and west tower. Plain 15th cent tower, rest rebuilt 1865. Norman pillars in arcade, but reconstructed. Traces of 13th cent work.

NOTE: Norman font; arcade; two bells in tower medieval 15th cent; early Victorian stained window; nearby is the holy well, with largest chapel in Cornwall, carefully restored 1897.

COLAN   D. St Colanus

Present church—chancel, nave, north aisle, south transept, porch and west tower, rebuilt in 19th cent. 13th cent church to which 15th cent aisle added. Restored 1884. Some old wood-work in screen base and roof.

NOTE: Brasses to John Cosowarth 1575, Frances Bluett 1572, with thirteen sons and nine daughters (no permission needed to rub, donation asked); memorials; portion of well-carved screen cut down; electrified oil lamps; sundial in porch; old woodwork in roof; one medieval bell 15th cent; ancient cross, recently discovered, by porch; old organ.

ST COLUMB MAJOR D. St Columba

Present church—chancel, nave, north and south aisles, north and south transepts, with arches into aisles, porches, parvises. Beer stone arcades. 15th cent tower (1433) stands on open arches at west end to allow access when buildings stood near. Old bench ends and some roof woodwork remain. Much destroyed in explosion 1676, including old glass. Many features not typically Cornish. Restorations in 1846, 1867 and later, with enrichments.

NOTE: Bench ends; modern plaque in baptistery; statues in north transept and Jesus chantry; window tracery of various styles; Arundell brasses (ask permission to rub) and slate memorials to members of the premier recusant family of Corn-wall; Italian lanterns in chancel; piscinas; old chest at west end; modern woodwork in screens, etc; carved panel of an-nunciation in Lady chapel.

Guide

ST COLUMB MINOR D. St Columba

Present church—chancel, nave, north and south aisles, porch and stately west tower. Font could be Norman or 15th cent copy. A font of genuine cable-moulded Norman date and style at Rialton possibly comes from here. Church mostly 14th and 15th cent, resored 1889. Some old woodwork remains. Modern screen at west end.

NOTE: Font; Royal Arms Charles II; piscinas; stained windows;

old chair; slate memorials to Elizabeth Pollamounter 1640, Roger Ellery 1640—with curious breeches! Screen at west end; sundial 1826.

Guide

CONSTANTINE   D. St Constantinus

Present church—chancel, nave, north and south aisles, second north aisle or chapel, porch and west tower, three stages. Large, spacious, 15th and 16th cent. Restorations in 19th cent. Some old woodwork left in part of screen.

NOTE: Brasses to Richard Gerveys 1574, a palimpsest with 14th cent Flemish knight on hidden side; another brass in Bosahan (north aisle), John Pendarves 1616 (ask permission to rub these); part of 15th cent roodscreen; monuments; windows; stoup; roodloft stairs; parish chest, carved panels c 1520; more than 200 kneelers embroidered with subjects connected with the parish (1960–); ring of bells augmented to six in 1958 by Taylors of Loughborough.

CORNELLY   D. St Cornelly

Present church—diminutive 13th cent chancel, nave, north aisle or chapel, small (leaning) tower at west end, porch. All restored in 19th cent by J. P. St Aubyn. A few bits of carved woodwork left in porch.

NOTE: 13th cent single light window in north nave wall; 15th cent window in nave; memorials and pulpit with painted panels; east stained windows; fireplace in Gregor chapel or aisle; chimney remains outside; head of Jane Gregor in white marble 1783; outside private door to chapel; Latin monument to Francis Gregor.

CRANTOCK   D. St Carantoc

Present church—chancel, chancel aisles, nave without aisles, transepts, porch, west tower. Chancel roof higher than nave roof. Once a collegiate church. Norman and cruciform, ex-

tended in 13th and 14th cent with central (or west?) tower.
This collapsed in 15th cent and another was built at west end.
College dissolved 1545. Much careful 19th and 20th cent restoration and enrichment by Edmund Sedding. Modern carved
screen, incorporating five pillars of medieval screen, with rood
figures.

NOTE: Norman (?) font, worked over and dated 1474; chancel
arch; 18th cent communion rails; stone altar in Lady chapel;
modern carved benches modelled on ancient examples; statue
of St Carantoc; fine screen; stained windows; return stalls;
ancient Saxon (?) stone coffin; stocks under shelter in churchyard.

Guide

CREED   D. St Crida

Present church—chancel, nave, north transept, 15th cent south
aisle, stone vaulted porch, three-stage west tower rebuilt in
18th cent. Probably a Norman church enlarged in 15th cent
when south aisle and west tower added. Restored 1904. Some
old woodwork in roof.

NOTE: Norman pillar piscina, and two others of later date;
square carved stone (Norman?) in porch; Royal Arms George
IV; part of screen; memorials; modern carved table in south
aisle; porch with granite ribs (cf Tregony); slate memorials to
Thomas and Henry Denys 1570, 1602; 13th cent font; almsbox; King Charles's Letter; commandments boards in belfry;
roodloft stairs; remains of black letter text on wall of transept;
fragments of old glass in windows; old woodwork in south aisle
roof; old bell on floor 1726; two medieval bells in tower c 1400;
good modern memorial in churchyard to George Johnstone
1960; old school.

CROWAN   D. St Crewenna

Present church—chancel, nave, north aisle 15th cent; south
aisle built probably early 18th cent; three-stage tower 15th

cent. Norman original probable. Capitals of pillars of north aisle have large projections with angels bearing shields. Original south aisle had Tuscan columns, rebuilt 19th cent in imitation gothic. 1872 restored by J. P. St Aubyn, member of the local family.

NOTE: Norman font; curious base with carved figures; brasses to deceased St Aubyns 1400-1599 (brass rubbing not permitted); memorial tablets, one by Adam; base of classical column from aisle in churchyard; slate headstone to Richard Tregeare 1668 in tower vestry with curious inscription.

CUBERT   D. St Cubertus

Present church—chancel, nave, north transept 14th cent; south aisle and south transept 15th cent; porch and west tower with spire. Norman origin attested by font; perhaps only nave and chancel. Tower and spire fell in storm 1848, now rebuilt. Restored by G. E. Street in 1852. Some old woodwork left in chancel and aisle roofs.

NOTE: Norman font of unusual design; font cover (Georgian?); recess in south transept; Willis organ, formerly at Lanhydrock; slate memorial to Arthur and Humphrey Laurence 1669, 1699; ancient 7th cent monumental stone with inscription embedded in exterior tower wall.

CUBY   D. St Cuby
(Tregony)

Present church—chancel, nave, north transept, south aisle, porch and west tower of two stages. Norman font is evidence that a church of that date stood here. All rebuilt in 1828, except 14th cent tower and 16th cent south porch (?) (cf Creed), perhaps an earlier porch brought at that time from ruins of St James's church, Tregony. Restored 1899. Some scraps of old bench ends in pulpit.

NOTE: Norman font; carved panels in pulpit; carved panel on sanctuary wall; modern painted panels on organ of St James, St Cuby and St Anne; memorial tablets; inscribed stone 6th cent (?)—the Cuby stone—west end south aisle exterior; angle buttresses to tower; sundial on porch; carved corbel over doorway; stone ribbed roof to porch.

Guide

CURY   D. St Corentin

Present church—chancel, nave, 14th cent south transept, 15th cent north aisle, porch and two-stage west tower. Normans erected a possibly cruciform church here. The doorway remains. Noteworthy 'squint' in local style supported on pillar with small window. Restored 1873. Some old woodwork survives.

NOTE: Norman font; Norman south door with tympanum; squint in chancel/transept angle; cross in churchyard; a former vicar, Rev Sandys Wason 1905–19, an unusual character, was deprived for his ritual practices.

DAVIDSTOW   D. St David

Present church—chancel, nave, north and south aisles, porch and west tower of three stages. Originally 15th cent but drastically restored and rebuilt 1875. A few old bench ends, one with bagpipe player.

NOTE: Porch; memorials; windows; bench ends; fragments of old glass; sundial in churchyard.

ST DAY   D. Holy Trinity

Present church is permanently closed owing to its dangerous condition caused by bad design and deterioration of the stone itself. It consists of rectangular nave with small apse for sanctuary, north and south aisles, a western porch surmounted by a turret with pinnacles. Erected 1828 in Gothic style and once containing galleries (removed 1930), the seating capacity being over a thousand. It was condemned 1956, and closed. A great medieval pilgrim shrine of the Holy Trinity once stood hereabouts; nothing remains except a pinnacle of the tower, now at Scorrier. Legend has it, however, that a north aisle window at Gwennap came from the chapel. The district became a mining centre of West Cornwall and was made parochial in 1853. The intention is to reduce the walls and make a memorial garden within the church plan for the burial of ashes.

NOTE: Waterloo Church Gothic details; two ranges of windows for galleries; headstones in churchyard reflecting mining activity and dangers; visit the modern church and centre across the road (1967), itself a centre of pilgrimage to the shrine of Our Lady of Walsingham.

ST DENNIS   D. St Dionisius

Present church—a rectangular building under one roof, and a north-west tower. A Norman church once stood here and its font remains in part. The 14th cent two-stage tower is from a later rebuilding and alone survives. All else was swept away in 1847, when the south arcade was thrown out (part is at Nanpean), windows and walls meddled with and a single gable barn-like structure achieved without benefit of ecclesiological principles. Double chancel windows at east end. No old woodwork. Care and modern furnishings have softened the harshness.

NOTE: Ship windvane to tower; ancient cross near porch; Royal Arms Queen Anne 1711; brightly coloured roof trusses; commandment boards; circular entrenchment, or dinas, with fine view, in which church stands; medieval bell 15th cent.

DEVORAN   D. SS John and Petroc

Present church—a neat apsed chancel and nave, porch and tower with small spire 1885, by J. L. Pearson, architect of the Cathedral.

NOTE: East end details; memorials to members of Phillpotts family; memorial to Lobb brothers, collectors of foreign plants, who rendered service to British horticulture; some shrubs collected in churchyard.

ST DOMINIC   D. St Dominica, and
St Dominic (1963)

Present church—chancel, nave, north and south aisles, porch and tower at west end. Nothing remains of the Norman church which stood here. A church was dedicated 1259, but what now exists is mostly 15th cent restored 1873. A unique feature is that the tower top is larger than the lower stage, resting on corbels. This top is 15th cent and the lower part 13th cent. 15th cent woodwork remains in roofs.

NOTE: Modern altar rails with good carving; organ with painted panels; tomb in south aisle to Sir Anthony Rous 1620, and his son Ambrose, strongly Parliamentarian family in Civil War; windows and memorials; piscinas; roodloft stairs.

DULOE   D. St Cuby

Present church—chancel, nave, north aisle, north transept, Colshull chapel, south transept, porch and tower of two stages at end of south transept, with conical roof. Interesting church, probably cruciform in 13th cent. Tower and a few traces remain of this date, such as window in south transept. In 15th cent enlargement took place on north side. An aisle was added, with a later chapel for the Colshull family, who were patrons. Effigy in this chapel Sir John Colshull 1483. Later still, north transept erected. All restored 1860–1.

NOTE: Norman font and another; Colshull chapel with fine 15th cent Caen stonework, especially vines on piers; effigy; slate memorials, one to Maria Arundell, and anagram: Man a dry laurel; a former rector was Rev Robert Scott, partner in production of the Greek Lexicon with Liddell; another rector, Rev Paul Bush, was here for 45 years and restored the church.

Guide

EGLOSHAYLE   D. St Petroc

Present church—chancel, nave, south aisle and part north aisle, porch and west tower of three stages. This fine 15th cent church replaced a Norman one, of which font survives. Restored 1867. Some old woodwork in south aisle roof.

NOTE: Norman font; 15th cent stone pulpit; memorials from 1520; windows; stone chancel 'screen' 1920; Molesworth monument bust 1735; catacleuse west door of tower; snakes carved on door jambs; shields on tower mouldings; ancient crosses in churchyard.

Washaway is a 19th cent chapel-of-ease, St Conan, which has a pre-Norman font from Lanteglos-by-Camelford, and a 16th cent German pulpit; Martin Luther is supposed to have used it.

EGLOSKERRY   D. St Keria

Present church—chancel, nave, 15th cent south aisle, north transept, porch and west tower 15th cent. There was once a Norman church, of which there are some remains in font, north wall and arch of transept, piscina and two tympana. Restored 1879, 1886.

NOTE: Norman font; two tympana (one in outside of north door, blocked); pillar piscina; effigy of knight; memorials to local families; a former vicar, Rev H. A. Simcoe 1822–63, was a man of various skills—printer, medico and writer; slate memorials to William Saltren 1742, John Carne 1624; helmet and gauntlets.

Guide

ST ENDELLION   D. St Endelienta

Present church—chancel, nave, north and south aisles, porch and west tower, all 15th cent. Plain Norman font shows an earlier church stood here. Sensitive restoration 1937–8 has enhanced the dignity of this church and remedied the earlier harsh treatment it received in 19th cent. Some old woodwork remains in bench ends and roofs, and there is much good modern woodwork, some of which was carved in the village.

This is the sole survival in Cornwall of a Collegiate church. The foundation of the College is of uncertain date; it was reconstituted 1265 with four prebendaries. It somehow survived the confiscations of 1545 and the Victorian destruction.

NOTE: Four prebendal stalls; Norman font; shrine, in catacleuse stone, of St Endelienta c 1400; stoup; pulpit from parts of Jacobean altar rail; roodloft stairs; bronze plaque on west wall; 18th cent ringers' rhymes, with pictures of ringers, in belfry; fragment of wall painting; modern font cover with Oberammergau Christus statue; old photograph of bearded Tractarian vicar; modern oak pews by local craftswoman; woodwork in roofs with angles; tombstone with matrices for lost brasses.

Guide

ST ENODER   D. St Enodorus

Present church—chancel, nave, north and south aisles, north transept, porch with parvise and west tower of three stages. Of the Norman church only the font remains, and in its place is the spacious 14th and 15th cent church. North aisle is 15th cent; south a century earlier. The tower was rebuilt in 1710 after the collapse of its predecessor in 1686. Old roofs in nave and aisles. Porch and south aisle wall have sculptured detail of figures, trefoils and panels. Restored 1870. Old bench ends and panels from former roodscreen in pulpit. Clear glass except in east window.

NOTE: Norman font, a bowl with four heads; 25 bench ends; screen; sundial, within the church for safety, dated 1766; slate memorial to Dorothy Tanner 1634; pulpit; Georgian (?) Royal Arms; tracery in north transept window; niches in north aisle wall.

Guide

ST ENODOC See under St Minver

ST ERME D. St Hermes

Present church—chancel, nave, north and south aisles, transepts, porch and tower at west end of three stages. Originally chancel, nave, south aisle and transept, with 15th cent west tower. Completely rebuilt in 1820 (except tower), the old arcade set up further south with 1820 copy on north side, and the whole put under one gable roof, though the old woodwork was retained in remodelled ceilings. Many pinnacles and buttresses were added in the style of the 15th cent tower. Porch erected 1961, with original Norman arch recovered from local farm. Good Norman font remains with a band of ornamentation to show what once stood here.

NOTE: Brass to Robert Trencreek 1594 (ask permission to rub); Royal Arms George IV 1821; wall memorial to Cornelius Cardew, pluralist rector and master of Truro Grammar School; modern east window; good modern woodwork c 1912; font.

ST ERNEY D. St Terninus

Present church—chancel, nave, north aisle and west tower of 14th and 15th cent. Modern porches. Originally a Norman church here. Restored 1872. No old woodwork.

NOTE: Norman font; commandment boards; modern stained glass; one of three bells is medieval c 1400 (inaccessible); slate memorial to Henry Hody 1636; arms of Earl of St Germans on north wall.

Nearby is ancient earthwork, and half a mile away the Holy Well of St Mark.

ST ERTH D. St Ercus

Present church—chancel, nave, north and south aisles, porch, all 15th cent; three-stage west tower 14th cent. Norman font survives from earlier building. Sensitively restored in 1873 by J. D. Sedding. Old woodwork remains in roofs.

NOTE: Norman square-panelled font; niche in porch; modern screens, etc; gable windows in roofs; memorials; ancient cross in churchyard; sculptured creatures at tower parapet angles; slate headstone to Roger Wearn, clockmaker, 1820.

ST ERVAN   D. St Hermes
Present church—chancel, nave, north and south transepts, porch and west tower. A cruciform church of 13th cent badly restored in 19th cent. Interesting as showing structure free from 15th cent additions. Tower, taken down in 19th cent, rebuilt in 1960s.

NOTE: 14th cent font; windows; slate memorials to William Pomeroy 1622; Richard Russel, Commonwealth minister, 1654; Richard Harvey 1666; one medieval bell 15th cent.

ST EVAL   D. St Uvelus
Present church—chancel, nave, north transept, south aisle; porches, and west tower. Norman cruciform building, enlarged in 14th and 15th cents. The tower fell in 1700 and was rebuilt 1727, Bristol merchants assisting with funds as this tower was an important landmark for their shipping. Restored by J. D. Sedding in 1889. Some old woodwork left in roofs, screen parts, bench ends.

NOTE: Norman font; Norman window in north wall; curious arches in arcade; bench ends; sundial on porch; roodloft stairs; screen.

ST EWE   D. St Ewa and All Saints
Present church—chancel, nave, south aisle, north transept; porch, west tower and spire. Norman font and parts of walls show a church of that date stood here. The arcade is late 14th cent, as is the tower. Restored 1881 by J. P. St Aubyn. Screen with coving and loft late 15th cent remains in situ.

NOTE: Norman font; screen details; 15th cent altar slab in chancel; floriations on piers; hatchments; bust by Rysbrack; coffin lid; bench ends in pulpit; stocks.

FALMOUTH   D. All Saints
Built 1887, by J. D. Sedding. Parochial 1924. Chancel, wide

nave with ambulatory and barrel roof, transepts, porches; high square pillars without capitals; great reredos; modern statues; good carved case to organ; marble and alabaster pulpit; blue prevailing in east windows.

FALMOUTH   D. King Charles the Martyr
Present church—chancel, nave, north and south aisles, organ transept, porches, west tower, broad and thin. Gothic-classical 1662, added to and enriched. Originally a square, enlarged eastwards.
NOTE: Arcades of granite classical columns; font and cover 1759; pulpit; ironwork in screens; portrait of King Charles I; tablet given by Netherland Protestant churches in gratitude for wartime hospitality; chairs (1842) and credence (1759); two marble columns and responds; gallery at back; Royal Arms Queen Anne 1707; silver and enamel churchwarden's staves (1967); double range of windows; good stained glass; picture; many interesting wall tablets.

Guide

FEOCK   D. St Feock (sometimes Feoca)
Present church—chancel, nave, north and south aisles, north transept, porch mainly 15th cent, detached tower of two stages 13th cent. Unusual catacleuse font, possibly Norman. Restored 1874. Old woodwork in pulpit panels, probably Flemish, c 1650.
NOTE: Norman (?) font; arcades; Victorian reredos and chancel partition; detached tower; pulpit; stocks; ancient cross in churchyard; two 15th cent medieval bells; said to be the last parish in which service was conducted in the Cornish language before its recent revival—Rev William Jackman administered the Sacraments in Cornish till at least 1640.

FORRABURY   D. St Symphorian
(Boscastle)
Present church—chancel, nave, north aisle, south chapel, porch

and west tower. Font remains of a Norman church erected here, and also traces in south wall of nave. Modern restorations render the dating of existing church doubtful, but probably 15th cent reworking of earlier material. Restored 1868. Old woodwork, only a few bench ends in pulpit and altar.

NOTE: Norman font; old carved panel in pulpit, etc; porch roof of two large slabs of granite; weather vane on tower in form of a fish; old cross in churchyard; this is the tower (rebuilt 1760) featured in Rev R. S. Hawker's poem 'The Silent Tower of Bottreaux'; there is still only one bell here.

FOWEY   D. St Fimbarrus

Present church—chancel, nave, north and south aisles, arched porch with parvise, and west tower of four stages. Catacleuse font, similar to those at Feock and Ladock; church now mostly 14th cent, later porch and extensions to aisles. Clerestory, and arcades without capitals, as at Lostwithiel. Restoration 1876. Old woodwork in roof of nave, pulpit, etc.

NOTE: Grand tower; Norman font; groined ceiling of unusual porch; arcades and clerestory; stoup; 18th cent ringers' rules; many monuments to sea-going and local worthies; Elizabethan pulpit 1601, made from cabin of Spanish galleon; modern chancel screen; brass of Alice Rashleigh 1591, and others (ask permission to rub); roodloft stairs; memorial windows; war memorial gates. In the muniment room of parvise are some old cannon balls found in the walls, probably from Civil War campaign of 1644.

Guide

FLUSHING   D. St Peter

Present church—chancel, nave, north porch. The chancel has an apse. Mock-Norman, erected 1842.

NOTE: Fragment of ancient sculpture; reredos; Burne-Jones/ Morris window; old cross in churchyard; Bible garden.

ST GENNYS   D. St Genesius

Present church—chancel, nave, north and south aisles, porch and west tower, mainly 14th and 15th cents. Norman, with lower part of tower and square panelled font surviving. Restored 1871 by J. P. St Aubyn; tower top sympathetically replaced by Edmund Sedding c 1900. Some old woodwork.

NOTE: Norman tower, arch, windows and font; north arcade Polyphant piers; bench ends in litany desk; picture over side altar; church chest; stoup; memorial to William Braddon, Commissioner for Courts of Trial in Commonwealth; a former vicar, Rev George Thomson 1732–82, was converted by a thrice-repeated dream; at first a keen supporter of Wesley who preached here, himself went about preaching in the open air in other parishes till censured by the bishop; complaints had been made about his 'circumforaneous vociferations' in 1744. Wesley gave him the last sacrament in 1782.

ST GERMANS   D. St Germanus

Present church—chancel, nave, south chapel and aisle, north organ transept, southwest porch and twin west towers. Cornwall's most noteworthy survival of Norman work. West front, with doorway of seven orders, main part of twin towers, supported on piers and arches within. Remains of still earlier stonework on inner face of west front. South chapel 14th cent, pilgrim shrine of relics of St Germanus. In 15th cent Norman south aisle widened and porch erected. North aisle, lean-to, was demolished 1803 to make family pew for Port Eliot; great east window of chancel stood further east at end of monastic chancel. This was claimed after the Dissolution by the Crown. Parishioners rebuilt part of arcade and set the east window in wall erected at east end of nave. This fell in 1592, but was re-erected in the present position; the old chancel lay beyond the present one. Little old woodwork.

NOTE: Almost every feature of this building; traces of pre-Norman masonry at west end; Norman font, arcades, piers, capitals, windows, tower bases, etc; south chapel; statue of St

Anthony; one old monastic choir stall; niches; sedilia and piscina; stone coffin in porch; monuments by Rysbrack 1722; windows; cope case; 18th cent list of Cornish bishops of Saxon days, when cathedral stood here.

GERMOE   D. St Germochus

Present church—chancel, nave, north aisle with chapel, south transept, porch, west tower of three stages, 14th and 15th cent on Norman base. Norman cruciform church, with 15th cent north aisle and south transept. Restored 1891.

NOTE: Norman font; crucifix over porch; stoup; windows; corbel heads; gable corbels in porch; St Germoe's chair in churchyard.

Guide

GERRANS   D. St Gerendus

Present church—chancel, nave, south aisle 15th cent, north transept, porch, two-stage west tower with spire. Norman font. Church rebuilt 14th and 15th cents, and again in 1849, with care, by William White, after a fire 1848. Some old woodwork, bench ends.

NOTE: Norman font; piscina; old woodwork in porch roof; bench ends; screen and font cover 1851; stoup; old cross in churchyard.

Guide

ST GLUVIAS   D. St Gluvias

Present church—chancel, nave, north and south aisles, porch and west tower of three stages flanked by vestries to which it communicates by open arches. A church was dedicated here in 1318, but there are no traces in the existing building earlier than 15th cent. It was 'Grecianised' in the 18th cent, extensively restored 1883, and transformed in the 1950s under Sir Ninian Comper. Some old monuments survive, but no old woodwork.

NOTE: Brass to Thomas Kyllegrew c 1484 (ask permission to rub); 17th cent memorials to local families; tablet in chancel to Rev John Penrose, vicar 1741–76, an earnest incumbent whose diary and letters survive in part; another, Rev William Temple, was an ancestor of two Archbishops of Canterbury; memorial in churchyard to Hornblower family, eminent engineers to Cornish mines in 18th and 19th cents. The parish has three churchwardens instead of two, one nominated by the mayor of Penryn. The bell of the Town Hall was rung to summon people to church led by the mayor, as the borough had no Anglican place of worship of its own before recent extension.

GODOLPHIN   D. St John Baptist
Present church—lofty chancel, nave, aisles and porch. Erected 1851 by J. P. St Aubyn.
NOTE: Ancient cross by porch; memorial windows, including one to priest who died from smallpox contracted from visiting a sick parishioner 1873.

GORRAN   D. St Goran
Present church—chancel, nave, south aisle, north transept, porch and stately west tower of three stages. Probably a Norman church, of which there are traces in lower part of transept arch. Now mainly 15th cent. Restored in 1874 by J. P. St Aubyn. Many old bench ends remain.
NOTE: Font, probably only a copy of Norman style; bench ends; chair in chancel; good 20th cent panelling and refurnishing; some old glass in aisle windows; brass (in frame, ask permission to rub) of unknown 16th cent lady; piscina.

Guide

Gorran Haven (D. St Just)
Curious 15th cent chapel with five-sided tower. Long secularised, restored to use 1885 by J. P. St Aubyn. Chancel, nave and tower. Daughter church to above.

NOTE: Piscina; old woodwork in communion rails; curious openings in walls; east window by Rev William Willimott, vicar of Quethiock 1878–88.

Guide

GRADE D. Holy Cross

Present church—chancel, nave and porch 1862. West tower of two stages 14th cent. Old church was Norman cruciform with 15th cent north chapel, squint as at Landewednack and small arches at roodscreen.

NOTE: Font probably 15th cent; Norman window in north wall; brasses to James Erisey 1522, and others (ask permission to rub); trefoil niche in porch; medieval bells c 1510; carved figure in churchyard.

GULVAL D. St Wolvela (?)

Present church—chancel, nave, north and south aisles, north transept, porch and west tower of three stages. 13th cent church remodelled at various periods. Transept rebuilt 1891. Restored by J. P. St Aubyn.

NOTE: 13th cent font; part Saxon cross; piscina and credence; modern screen; memorials and windows; 14th cent cherub's head; Victorian woodwork, marble and brasswork; old bell; figures supporting tower pinnacles; sundial on porch. A former vicar, Rev William Wriothesley Wingfield, was presented as an ailing young man in 1839. He died in 1913, still in harness, having restored his church in his 73½ years' incumbency.

GUNWALLOE D. St Winwaloe

Present church—chancel, nave, north and south aisles, porch and detached west tower of two stages with pyramidal cap. Norman church here of which a broken font remains. Now mostly 14th and 15th cent. Restored 1869, when chancel and windows rebuilt. Old woodwork in south aisle and porch roofs and part of screen early 16th cent.

GWENNAP

NOTE: Norman font; good 20th cent woodwork; panelled jambs to porch doorway; detached tower; old cross in churchyard; tomb in churchyard—'We shall die all', with variations like bell changes; sea girt situation, causing anxiety. Marconi attended this church in early 20th cent while experimenting with radio at nearby Poldhu.

GWENNAP D. St Weneppa

Present church—chancel, nave, north and south aisles, porches Detached tower of two stages with ring of six bells, conical roof. 15th cent but retains little of interest except memorials to mine adventurers and workers. Restored between 1862 and 1891.

NOTE: Roodloft stairs; piscina; sundial 1773; tablet on north wall to James Whitburn carved by Nevill Northey Burnard at the age of 15; base of ancient font; ancient cross near northern entrance to church.

GWINEAR D. St Wineus or Fingar

Present church—chancel, nave, north and south aisles, north (Arundell) chapel, porch, west tower of three stages (15th cent). Normans had a church here, and part of the font is of that period. Most of the present building is 13th and 14th cent. Restored 1881. Old woodwork in pulpit, stalls and part of screen c 1510.

NOTE: Part of ancient font, bowl 1727; beak heads in porch; corbel heads in tower wall; panels in pulpit, one showing a merman; screen; stalls; five-light east window; piscina; marble memorial to Elizabeth Arundell 1683; old cross in churchyard; doorway by porch into chapel.

GWITHIAN D. St Gothian

Present church—chancel, nave, transepts, porch, west tower of three stages. Norman font bowl suggests a church of that date here. All rebuilt on smaller scale 1866, except 15th cent tower.

NOTE: Font bowl; sedilia; piscina; monuments; lychgate from part of excluded south aisle; old cross in churchyard.

St Gothian's Oratory lies buried in sand some way away. It consists of chancel and nave, similar to but larger than St Piran's Oratory at Perranporth.

HALSETOWN　D. St John Evangelist
Present church—chancel, nave, lean-to north and south aisles, south porch and saddle-back roofed west tower. Built 1866 by J. P. St Aubyn.
NOTE: Wood roof timbers in nave; clerestory; chancel screen with apostles (faces of local personalities, one who refused to pay left bald!), 19th cent stained windows; local artist's work; medallion of St John the Evangelist; in churchyard, conservation park and open-air altar.

Guide

HAYLE　D. St Elwyn
Present church—chancel, nave with clerestory, north chapel, north and south aisles, porch and tower with short spire and lantern, on north side. Built 1886–8 by J. D. Sedding. An interesting Victorian church in a mixture of styles. One of Sedding's last and best works. Not Cornish in atmosphere, but dignified and stately.
NOTE: Gallery from tower into church; chancel iron gates.

HELLAND　D. St Helen (?)
Present church—chancel, nave, short south aisle, north transept, porch and west tower. A reconstructed church by J. P. St Aubyn (?) leaving arcade to 15th cent south chapel alone to declare antiquity. A few traces might be 13th cent. Transept has 1646 on gable; altered c 1820 as a day school and cut off from church. Now a vestry. Restored and tower rebuilt 1883.
NOTE: Slate memorial to Humfrey Calwodely early 16th cent; tubular bells in belfry, chimed from a frame; detail of Charles I's gift to a church of cloak for altar frontal; fragments of old glass; memorials and windows.

HELSTON   D. St Michael

Present church—chancel, nave, porch and west tower of three stages. An earlier church, with chancel, nave, aisles and tower with spire, was badly damaged in a storm about 1727. In 1761 a new rectangular classical church was erected. Later a chancel and tower were added, and galleries in 1837. Reordered with removal of galleries, etc and installation of central altar 1971.
NOTE: Font; Victorian reredos; brass to Thomas Bougies 1602 (not possible to rub); other memorials; modern screen; great chandelier 1763; old cross in churchyard; sundial 1792.

HERODSFOOT   D. All Saints

Present church—chancel, nave, porch and gable turret. Built 1850. Early last century this area was thickly populated with silver-lead mining. Mining closed down in 1860s, but manufacture of explosives carried on till 1963, when an accident brought it to an end.
NOTE: Norman font, from old chapel of St Martin in Respryn, St Winnow parish. Bowl form with band of ornament.

HESSENFORD   D. St Anne

Present church—chancel, nave, lean-to north and south aisles, porch and slender bell turret and fleche. By G. E. Street in lancet style. Rebuilt 1871.
NOTE: Organ case; memorial windows; choir stalls; pulpit; lectern; prominent site.

ST HILARY   D. St Hilary

Present church—chancel, nave, transepts, choir aisles, north and south aisles, porch, by William White 1853, and the old west tower and spire. A fire in 1853 destroyed the 15th cent church, except for the tower and spire, lower part of which is 13th cent.
NOTE: North doorway a 15th cent survival; old font; tower base 13th cent; Roman milestone found in church walls; crosses and priests' tomb in churchyard; choir stalls with early 20th cent

paintings of saints by local artists; remains of altar reredos from incumbency of Rev Bernard Walke, famous and loved vicar 1912–32.

ILLOGAN   D. St Illogan

Present church—chancel, nave, north and south aisles and porch. Originally a church with chancel, nave and tower of 14th cent. In 1846 a new church on a new site. The tower remains apart and has angle buttresses; it contains a ring of six bells.

NOTE: Brass to James Bassett 1603 (ask permission to rub); memorials from old church; Jacobean panels in pulpit; slate memorial to George Hele 1706; no west doorway in tower; bust of Francis Bassett 1835 by Westmacott; memorial to Rev Dr John Collins 1684; rectors' list with four Collins' 1435–1684; old chairs in chancel; old cross in churchyard.

THE ISLES OF SCILLY

ST MARY

Old church—Norman arch and pillar show a church of that date stood here. Present edifice (1891) only a portion of later building which was extended in 17th cent and now used for mortuary purposes and occasional services.

HUGH TOWN   D. St Mary

Present church—chancel, nave, west tower. Erected 1834 (instigated by William IV)–1837.

NOTE: Wooden lion from *Association* wrecked 1707; good stained windows; Willis organ; painting by Reni Guido, 16th cent Italian artist, of St Joseph and the child Jesus; cisterns on terrace dated 1727.

TRESCO   D. St Nicholos

Present church—chancel, nave, transepts, north porch and tower at west end. Erected 1879.

NOTE: Memorial windows; priory ruins.

ST AGNES   D. St Agnes
Present church—nave and western tower 1827.
NOTE: St Warna's well 6th cent.

BRYHER   D. All Saints
Present church—nave and turret 1742.

ST MARTINS   D. St Martin
1866.

ST HELENS
Remains of Celtic oratory, St Elidius, 7th cent or earlier.

Guide

ST ISSEY   D. St Issey
Present church—chancel, nave, north and south aisles, porch and west tower all rebuilt after collapse of tower in 1869. Many features of old church incorporated.
NOTE: Important 15th cent catacleuse details, west door; stoup; reredos (patiently pieced from broken fragments); photo of policeman in top hat on collapsed tower; 14th cent pieta in Lady chapel; font, late Norman, has date 1664 when replaced after Commonwealth.

ST IVE   D. St Ivo
Present church—chancel, nave, north transept, south aisle, porch and west tower. Considerable evidence of 14th cent church which had chancel, nave and north transept. Late 15th cent south aisle and porch. 16th cent tower with three stages, built traditionally by munificence of Henry Trecarrel of Lezant. Restored 1883 by Medley Fulford. Old woodwork remains in roofs.
NOTE: Elaborate 14th cent details at east end: five-light east window, niches, sedilia, piscina; pulpit 1700; Royal Arms Charles II 1660; (slate memorial to Blanche and John Wrey

1597, taken to Tawstock, Devon); sundial 1695; tower with clusters of pinnacles and double buttressed; stocks.

Guide

ST IVES D. St Ia

Present church—chancel, nave, north and south aisles, with additional south or Trenwith aisle, porch and four-stage grand west tower. Traces of 14th cent work in font, but largely 15th cent. Restoration various times in 19th cent. Much old woodwork in roofs, bench ends, angels at junctions of rafters and wall plates. Original screen with organ was broken up by Puritans 1647.

NOTE: 15th cent font; brass to Otho Trenwith 1646 (ask permission to rub); bench ends and panels of seat given by Ralph Clies, master smith; poppy heads; shields with name of John Peyn, mayor, executed 1549; Jacobean panels in pulpit; statue of Virgin and Child by Barbara Hepworth; baptistry designed by S. Dykes Bower 1956; arcade to Trenwith aisle carved with vines (cf Duloe); corbel heads on outside of south aisle; memorial windows; chancel roof with extra elaboration; old cross in churchyard.

Guide

JACOBSTOW D. St James

Present church—chancel, nave, north and south aisles, porch and west tower of three stages. Norman font remains in a largely 15th cent church. Restored 1887 and enriched since. Old woodwork remains in roofs, bench ends built into pulpit.

NOTE: Norman font, with curious dragon heads; Elizabethan altar table; pulpit; chest; roodloft stairs; ancient altar in Lady chapel replaced 1971; aumbry in Lady chapel; stoup—Celtic font (?); memorial stone in vestry to John Wells, famous Oxford mathematician; six bells re-hung 1970; ornamented band at base of tower.

ST JOHN   D. St John Evangelist
Present church—chancel and nave, rebuilt 1868 by William
White, porch 1605, west tower, two stages, late Norman.
NOTE: Lancet window in tower, similar to that at St Gennys;
15th cent font; chandelier; medieval bell 15th cent (in-
accessible).

ST JULIOT   D. St Julitta
Present church—chancel, nave, north aisle, porch with groined
roof, and tower of three stages at west end of present north aisle.
Restoration and rebuilding, including tower, in 1872 by
Thomas Hardy the writer, then in G. R. Crickmay's architectural office. He married the rector's sister-in-law. The old
nave and chancel were replaced by the present smaller north
aisle and the 15th cent former south aisle became the nave and
chancel. Thus the tower is now at the west end of the new small
north aisle. The north transept was destroyed at this time, with
much old woodwork and a Jacobean pulpit. The only old
woodwork surviving is in the wallplate of the present nave and
chancel.
NOTE: Memorial to Hardy, and another to his wife; groined
roof to porch (cf Tregony, Creed); old woodwork in wall-
plates of present nave and chancel (old south aisle); Victorian
screen and pulpit; ancient crosses in churchyard; snowdrops
in February worth seeing; old font bowl in churchyard.

ST JUST-IN-PENWITH D. St Just
Present church—chancel, nave, north and south aisles, porch
and west tower of three stages. An earlier cruciform church
stood here, but now chiefly 15th cent. Chancel rebuilt 1834,
part of south wall originally 14th cent. Restored by J. P. St
Aubyn in 1866.
NOTE: Ancient pillar stone with Chi-Rho monogram 5th cent (?);
well-sculptured capitals; arches of different spans; flamboyant
tracery of east windows; piscina; sedilia; wall paintings of
Christ of the Trades and of St George and the dragon; chan-

delier 1746; 8th or 9th cent cross shaft in north wall; roodloft stairs; rough interior masonry; two medieval bells; sundial; a former vicar George Cornelius Gorham, 1846–50, was a central figure in a famous controversy in early Victorian times.

Guide

ST JUST-IN-ROSELAND D. St Just

Present church—chancel, chancel aisle, nave, south aisle, north transept, porch and west tower of three stages 13th to 15th cents. Much visited for its beautiful setting. Pews and pulpit installed by Rev C. W. Carlyon, Victorian rector, amateur architect and craftsman (see St Anthony-in-Roseland). Restored 1872. Old woodwork in porch roof.

NOTE: Rare double piscina; panelled jambs to porch; brass of vested priest c 1520 (ask permission to rub); roodloft stairs; 15th cent font; 17th cent font cover; creed and Lord's Prayer panels 1693. Adornment of churchyard.

Chapelry of St Mawes rebuilt 1881.

ST KEA   D. St Keus; All Hallows

Present church—chancel, nave, north and south aisles, south transept, west tower with spire by G. Fellowes Prynne. Original church was at Old Kea, largely 15th cent. In 1803 this was pulled down (except the tower, which remains by the river) and a church by Wyatt erected 1802. This was replaced by present spacious church in 1895.

NOTE: Norman font, from old church; modern woodwork; memorial windows; 16th cent French chalice and paten (not accessible); shaft of old cross in churchyard; medieval bell 15th cent; chapelry at Old Kea 1863; tower of old church.

KENWYN   D. St Keyne

Present church—chancel, nave, north and south transepts, south aisle, porch and three-stage west tower. A 13th cent church so drastically altered and restored that its stages of development are obscure. South aisle is 15th cent. Tower shows 14th and 15th cent details. Restored 1820 and 1862, and by J. P. St Aubyn, who installed the alabaster reredos. Recent reordering and new seating and enrichment. No old woodwork. NOTE: 13th cent (?) carved head in south wall near tower; reredos; fireplace in south transept; stained windows; tapestry; Powell memorial in north transept; good modern pews and stalls 1960–4; lychgate house, once a school; ancient well in churchyard; musical ring of bells—in 18th cent a 'ringing club' for gentlemen of Cornwall existed here and the great 'squire Lemon' was a member. Still much enthusiasm here for ringing; Rev Richard Milles, vicar, entertained Rev John Wesley 1787.

Guide

ST KEVERNE   D. St Akeveranus
Present church—chancel, nave, north and south aisles, west porch and engaged west tower of two stages and spire. Rededication 1266, but now mostly late 15th cent with traces of 13th cent construction re-used. Restored 1893 by Edmund Sedding, and since enriched. Much old woodwork in roofs and bench ends.
NOTE: Font; three sets of roodloft stairs, all contemporary—a mystery; tower arches; painting of St Christopher; bench ends; many memorials to shipwrecked men; base of cross, part of original roodscreen dated 1457; statue of saint in niche above door; Jacobean pulpit; old chests; chancel window memorial to 100 drowned at loss of SS *Mohegan* 1898; ring of eight bells 1907.

ST KEW   D. St James
Present church—chancel, nave, north and south aisles, porch with three-stage west tower from 14th cent. Stately late 14th and 15th cent building, no apparent traces of earlier structures known to exist here. Restored 1883. Some old woodwork in roofs and a few bench ends.

NOTE: Old glass in north and south aisle east windows; slender arcades with ornamented capitals; lantern head of cross in catacleuse stone; 14th cent font; Jacobean pulpit; slate memorial to Honor Webber 1601; Royal Arms Charles II 1661; good Victorian screen 1883 and stalls; long chancel; old ox yoke at back of church; one window of belfry stage of tower glazed; roodloft stairs; ancient cross by churchyard entrance.

ST KEYNE   D. St Keyne

Present church—chancel, nave, short north aisle, plain 15th cent piers, south transept or vestry, porch and west tower. Hood moulding over door with three heads indicates a Norman church stood here. Damaged by ruthless restoration by J. P. St Aubyn, 1868–77. No old woodwork left.

NOTE: Norman hoodmoulding over door; 15th cent font; west aisle window 14th cent; old communion table in vestry; medieval bell 15th cent.

KILKHAMPTON   D. St James

Present church—chancel, nave, north and south aisles, porch and west tower of three stages. Striking Norman door of four orders only survival of church of that period. Present church is 15th cent. Restored 1860 under Sir Gilbert Scott. Much old woodwork remains. Good screenwork of 1860 period.

NOTE: Norman south doorway; inscription Porta Coeli 1567; rich bench ends and stalls; Victorian woodwork; screens; font with inverted inscription 16th cent; statue of St James; Royal Arms Charles II 1660; slate memorial with figures to Sarah Cottell 1727; memorials to Grenvilles, notable in Cornish history; others, some by Michael Chuke, a local and pupil of Grinling Gibbons; bronze equestrian figure on memorial; organ, part of which is 17th cent, keyboard preserved.

Guide

LADOCK   D. St Ladoca

Present church—chancel, nave, south aisle and short north

aisle or Trethurffe chapel, porch and noble tower of three stages at west end. Formerly a cruciform church, enlarged in 15th cent when south aisle and tower were added. Restored in 1864 by G. E. Street. Some old woodwork in 15th cent south aisle roof and 16th cent lower part of screen.

NOTE: Late Norman font of catacleuse stone; screen and roof woodwork; small slate tablet to William Randell, gent, amateur horologist; slate memorial to Nicholas Cornelius of Ladock 1632; stocks; organ by Willis; Victorian brasswork in standard candelabra, etc; Burne-Jones and Morris windows 1864; bishop's chair formerly belonging to Lord Rodney; carved stone at east end of churchyard wall.

LAMORRAN   D. St Moran

Present church—chancel, nave, north and south transepts, porch and small detached tower. Cruciform church of 13th cent drastically restored by amateurs in 1845, 1853.

NOTE: Detached tower; slate memorials with figures to Mary Verman 1665, John and Catherine Verman 1666; font, possibly Norman refashioned, in catacleuse stone; fragments of old glass; old cross in churchyard.

LANDEWEDNACK   D. St Winwaloe

Present church—chancel, nave, north aisle, south transept, groined porch and west tower of granite and serpentine, two stages, without buttresses. Fine Norman doorway shows a church of that date stood here. 14th cent tower, porch and some windows, but mostly 15th cent. Restored 1860. Some old woodwork.

NOTE: Norman south doorway; font, with inscription: D:RIC BOLHAM ME FECIT (rector 1404–15); squint to altar from transept, supported on a column, small window to light it, in a local style; pulpit; bench ends in desk; old woodwork in roofs; piscinas; stoup; three medieval bells (inaccessible); groined roof to porch; bell in churchyard.

LANDRAKE   D. St Michael (St Peter?)
Present church—chancel, nave, north aisle, south transept, porches and stately west tower of three stages, with stair turret and buttresses. Part of Norman nave and sanctuary, with doorway, remains. The rest is chiefly 15th cent enlargement. Restored 1877, and enriched since.
NOTE: Norman doorway and font; fine brass to Edward Courtenay 1500 (ask permission to rub); piscina; unusual chancel arch of wood; 17th cent slate memorials; window to roodloft stairs, opening into chancel; screens 1905; alabaster reredos, Victorian.

LANDULPH   D. SS Leonard and Dilp
Present church—chancel, nave, north and south aisles, porch and west tower of three stages. There are traces of Norman and other early construction in tower door jambs, base of font, and lower courses of walls. Chiefly 15th cent. Much good woodwork remains, including 15th cent bench ends, and has been completed or added to successfully in modern times.
NOTE: Font c 1200, bears date 1660, when replaced after Commonwealth; arcades; Lower seats 1630; slate memorial in tower to FitzAnthony Pennington; important brass to Theodore Palaelogus 1636 (ask permission to rub); roodloft stairs; Royal Arms George IV; marble tomb Sir Nicholas Lower; part figure in porch niche; memorial to Rev F. Jago-Arundell, early 19th cent rector and antiquary; situation at river's edge.

LANEAST   D. St Sidwell
Present church—chancel, nave, south aisle, north transept, porch and west tower of three stages. A Norman cruciform church remodelled in 14th and 15th cents. Restored 1850. Old woodwork in roofs, screens and bench ends.
NOTE: Norman font; old woodwork in screen c 1500; 38 bench ends and roofs; 15th cent glass in east window; 13th cent window in north transept; memorial to John Couch Adams, discoverer of planet Neptune; pulpit 16th cent—Rev John

LANHYDROCK

Wesley preached here in mid-18th cent; stocks; stoup; ancient cross in churchyard. Nearby is the holy well with 16th cent enclosure.

Guide

LANHYDROCK   D. St Hydroc

Present church—chancel, nave, north and south aisles, porch and west tower. Mostly 15th cent restored in 19th cent. No ancient woodwork survives except in porch roof.

NOTE: Window embrasures on south side like closed doors; hatchment; Royal Arms James I 1621; alabaster reredos; memorials to Robartes family members; ancient bell, recast 14th cent, with inscription ATHELSTAN SUMPTA ANIMA SUA (inaccessible) reversed; good woodwork and furnishings in Victorian prosperous style; cross in churchyard.

Attached to Lanhydrock House, now National Trust, by private path.

LANIVET   D. Unknown

Present church—chancel, nave, north and south aisles, porch and stately west tower of three stages. Mostly 15th cent building with no traces of earlier work. All old woodwork restored away, in 1864. A wall painting of Christ of the Trades was discovered at that time, but could not then be preserved.

NOTE: Norman capital brought from Bodmin Priory (?); inscription to Rev John Cody, former rector, 1485; fragments of old glass in north aisle windows; roodloft stairs; slate memorials to John and Richard Courtney 1559, 1632; Victorian reredos; communion plate is kept in 14th cent leather box (not accessible to view); ancient crosses and coped stone in churchyard.

LANLIVERY   D. St Bryvyth

Present church—chancel, nave, north transept and south aisle, porch and stately west tower of three stages, in a commanding situation. Scanty traces attest the existence of a Norman church.

Originally cruciform and possibly 14th cent, the erection of the 15th cent south aisle was accompanied by other remodelling and the construction of the tower. Restored 1878–91. Old woodwork in south aisle and porch roofs.

NOTE: Fragments of Norman font; 15th cent alabaster of the Resurrection; roodloft stairs; original hinges to south door; good woodwork in south aisle roof and porch roof; memorials to members of Kendall family of Pelyn, prominent in Cornish history; ringers' rhymes and picture in tower 1811; corbelled upper stage of tower supported by angels, lions and human heads; large granite blocks comprising tower; stone coffin.

LANNER   D. Christ Church
(Lanarth)

Present church—chancel, nave, south aisle, north porch, all plain and unadorned, 1845. South aisle 1883.

NOTE: Ancient crosses in churchyard; font, formerly in St Dunstan's, Fleet Street, London—possibly an old one.

LANREATH D. SS Marnarch and Dunstan

Present church—chancel, nave, south aisle, north transept, porch and west tower of three stages. The font and traces in the north transept show a Norman church stood here. In the succeeding 14th and 15th cents the building was remodelled and the south aisle and tower built. The church is noteworthy for the careful restoration it has received and the splendid array of woodwork it contains. The screen has lost its coving, but has painted panels in the lower part, which have been restored.

NOTE: Norman font; fragment of Norman altar slab; Royal Arms Charles II 1660; Elizabethan pulpit; Grylls monument with figures under canopy, all in wood and remarkable, 1623; fine screen, with painted lower panels; carved seat fronts in Lady chapel; turnedwood chair; niche and statue corbels in porch; ringers' rules c 1750; King Charles's Letter; Jacobean font cover; stocks; sundial 1828; ringing certificates in tower; roodloft stairs; woodwork in roofs.

LANSALLOS   D. St Ildierna

Present church—chancel, nave, south aisle, short north aisle, porch, and tower of three stages at west end. Norman font bowl, square with panelled sides, shows a building of that date stood here. Traces of 13th cent work, but mostly 15th cent. Restored 1883–4 and since. A good deal of ancient woodwork in roofs, benches, etc.

NOTE: Norman font; effigies of knight and lady (?); slate memorial with figures to Margery Budockshide 1579; 34 bench ends, one with three faces, symbolic of Trinity (?); Jacobean wardrobe; pulpit base from fallen tower pinnacle 1923; pre-Reformation bell 15th cent.

LANTEGLOS-BY-CAMELFORD
D. St Julitta

Present church—chancel, nave, south aisle, north transept, porch and west tower of three stages, unbuttressed and 15th cent. Traces of Norman cruciform church in north walls of nave and chancel. Usual 15th cent south aisle and font. Harshly restored 1872. Old woodwork in roofs and some other scraps.

NOTE: 15th cent font; fragments of old glass in apex of windows; old woodwork in roofs; niche and stoup in south doorway; unusual tracery in east window of chancel; south doorway, floriations in hollows of moulding; fragments of stone tracery, etc and windows of early form at back of church; interesting inlaid case of organ said once to be property of George III; closed priest's door on outside of north chancel wall; old crosses and Anglo-Saxon pillar with inscription in churchyard; sundial 1719. A former 18th cent rector, Rev Daniel Lombard, a Huguenot, left a library of now unreadable theological books; some humorous legends about him survive.

Guide

St Thomas of Canterbury, Camelford chapel-of-ease, 1938, is beautiful and well appointed, with a simple chancel, nave, south transept and vestry.

LANTEGLOS-BY-FOWEY
D. St Wyllow

Present church—chancel, nave, north and south aisles, south chancel aisle, porch and west tower partly engaged and of three stages. Norman work in tower arches, door jambs; 14th cent arcade of wide span; 15th cent south arcade. Carefully restored by E. Sedding 1904–5. Old woodwork remains in roofs, pews and bench ends. Much later careful restoration and enrichment.

NOTE: 13th cent font; piers and arcades; tower arches; brass to Sir Thomas de Mohun 15th cent, another to John and Anne Mohun 1507 (ask permission to rub); roodloft stairs; fine bench ends; pews with fine panels of Jacobean woodwork against walls; altar table inscribed 'the gift of Baranet Mohun to the Parishe 1634'; two Elizabethan table legs supporting credence; piscina; alabaster of martyrdom of St Lawrence; Royal Arms of Charles II 1668; Jacobean sideboard; black-letter commandment boards; old sketches 1903 of unrestored church; statue of St Wyllow; fragments of old glass; tablecloth with visitors' signatures; sundial; lantern cross; stocks.

Polruan had an ancient public chapel of St Saviour which has disappeared except for one massive fragment of the tower. A modern chapel-of-ease continues the name and function.

LAUNCELLS   D. St Swithin
Present church—chancel, nave, north and south aisles, porch and west tower of three stages. Mutilated Norman font may show a church of that date stood here. But present spacious, lofty building is mainly of 15th cent. North arcade is granite, south is Polyphant. Unrestored and carefully tended, a wealth of old woodwork and also Georgian fittings.

NOTE: Norman font; 15th cent floor tiles in chancel; old roofs; stoup; benches and about 60 bench ends of superior design; panelling; wall painting of Abraham sacrificing Isaac; old chest; tomb with effigy 1624; Royal Arms Charles II; sounding board over pulpit; Georgian box pews; modern screen to tower; semi-circular communion rails; reredos 1720; organ 1971; in churchyard is buried Sir Goldsworthy Gurney (1875), inventor of incandescent lighting and the steam jet. The team of ringers who rang in 1760 at George III's accession rang again at his jubilee in 1810. Rev R. S. Hawker's poem, 'The Ringers of Launcells Tower', is on this theme.

Guide

LAUNCESTON D. St Mary Magdalene

Present church—chancel, nave, north and south aisles, south porch with parvise, and detached tower at west end. Tower is from a 14th cent building. The present church is large, stately and 16th cent (1511–24), all of which (except tower) is covered externally with carved granite facing, traditionally the benefaction of Henry Trecarrel of Lezant after the untimely death of his infant son and heir. Between church and tower is now a vestry, but at one time two cottages.

NOTE: Pulpit, early 16th cent, carefully restored 1971; Royal Arms George I; 18th cent front to organ; 17th and 18th cent monuments; Piper monument 1731; brass to an unknown woman c 1630 (ask permission to rub); chairs in sanctuary; screens 1911 and other modern woodwork; reredos; Latin text along frieze of outer walls; arms of Henry VIII at apex of chancel window. This tower housed the first public clock in Cornwall in 1433 (not the present movement).

Guide

LAUNCESTON D. St Thomas the Apostle

Present church—chancel, nave, south aisle, vestry on north side, north porch and west tower of two stages. The massive font and the tympanum in the porch wall are Norman, but could have come from elsewhere, probably the priory church nearby after its suppression. The church as it stands is largely

14th and 15th cent. Restored. Old woodwork in tower screen, possibly from former roodscreen.

NOTE: Norman font of Polyphant stone; Norman tympanum with circular designs and the Agnus Dei; remains of wall paintings; tower screen; carved stone with St Catherine's wheel; piscina; ruins of the priory alongside the church.

LAWHITTON   D. St Michael

Present church—chancel, nave, south aisle, south porch and tower of three stages at centre of south side. Norman tower base and font remain from a church of that period, possibly cruciform. The outlines cannot be traced now owing to rebuilding at various periods. The south aisle is 15th cent, and the tower completed in 13th and 15th cent. Restored 1860 and 1873 by J. D. Sedding. A little old woodwork remains in porch roofs and a few benches with bench ends.

NOTE: Norman font; tower base of same period; seven benches and bench ends; fine old tiles in chancel; stone altar; pulpit dated 1663, attractive corner brackets; stoup; 17th cent almsbox; White House near lychgate, former 'palace' of bishops of Exeter, has 'mitre' chimneystack.

LELANT   D. St Uny

Present church—chancel, nave, north and south aisles, porch and west tower of three stages, buttressed. Part of an original Norman arcade survives, the capitals displaying scallop ornament. The remainder of the church is early and late 15th cent. This church is the mother church of St Ives, Towednack and Carbis Bay. All now separate parishes. Restored 1873. Old woodwork in roof of south aisle.

NOTE: Norman font bowl, rediscovered in a farmyard and restored 1889; Norman arch and piers in north arcade; Jacobean altar now in Lady chapel; roodloft stairs; 15th cent catacleuse doorway in north wall; slate memorials to William Praed 1620, Stephen Pawley 1635, Judith and Hugh Pawley 1698,

1721; stoup; sundial on porch; ancient crosses in church-yard.

Guide

LESNEWTH   D. St Michael and All Angels
Present church—chancel, nave, small remodelled south chapel used as a vestry, porch and 15th cent west tower of three stages. Only the tower and a few fragments remain from before the reconstruction of this church in 1862 by J. P. St Aubyn. His plan remains on the wall, framed. Transepts were removed and all old woodwork cleared out. A 'Norman' (?) window with altar slab as its sill is sited in north wall of chancel.
NOTE: Little window in aumbry on south side of chancel; altar slab with crosses in north window; some Norman stone in solitary pier of chapel aisle; new chancel arch; old cross in churchyard and relics of old stone tracery, etc discarded at restoration; features of J. P. St Aubyn's handiwork in crested tiling on ridge; iron gable cross; pitchpine and open roofs within; scraper at porch entrance.

ST LEVAN   D. St Selevan
Present church—chancel, nave, south aisle, north transept, porch and two-stage west tower. A Norman building, completely reconstructed by 15th cent, leaving only the font and stoup. Restored 1876. Old woodwork in screen panels, bench ends.
NOTE: Norman font; stoup; many good bench ends, picturing pilgrim with staff, etc; piscina; roodloft stairs; screen, restored; pulpit, inlaid, with date 1752; arcade to transept indicates intention to erect an aisle; crosses in churchyard; holy well and hermitage; St Levan's stone.

Guide

LEWANNICK   D. St Martin of Tours
Present church—chancel, nave, north and south aisles, porch

and tower at west end of three stages. The Norman font is evidence that a church of that date stood here. 15th cent rebuilding obliterated all traces of previous work. In 1890 the whole church and tower were gutted by fire and all woodwork, some of it excellent, was destroyed, except a few pieces in the porch. Rebuilding involved the erection of a new south arcade in the local Polyphant stone and extensive repair of the north arcade.

NOTE: Norman font; cresset stone, primitive form of lighting; Ogham stones 6th cent; carved panels in soffit of tower; odd transoms in windows; photographs of fire-damaged church; old chest early 17th cent.

LEZANT   D. St Briochus

Present church—chancel, nave, north and south aisles, porch and tower at west end of three stages, buttressed. There are hints of Norman work at the east end in chancel walls and the west wall of north aisle, where a window shows characteristics of the period. The font (said to have been defaced by Roundheads) is recut from a Norman original. The rest of the building is 15th cent, though traces of 14th cent work appear in the porch doorway. Restored 1869. The roofs contain the only old woodwork.

NOTE: Recut Norman font; piscina and modern aumbry in south aisle; piscina and aumbry in chancel; roodloft stairs; slate tomb chest to Thomas Trefusis 1606 in south aisle; 16th and 17th cent memorials; memorial windows.

Trecarrel and chapel may also be seen, built by Henry Trecarrel whose munificence enriched the churches of St Mary Magdalene, Launceston, Linkinhorne and St Ive. He was buried in Lezant church, where organ now stands.

LINKINHORNE   D. St Melor

Present church—chancel, nave, south aisle, 16th cent porch, north aisle and splendid west tower of four stages, buttressed, being traditionally the benefaction of Henry Trecarrel of Lezant. There is a Norman font, but all the rest is late 15th and 16th cent. Restored 1891, and since enriched. A little old woodwork and stained glass.

NOTE: Late Norman font; south porch doorway with ornamental carving and other features; old altar stone; wall paintings, Christ of the Trades; bench ends; memorial windows and tablets; tower arch and modern tower screen; stocks; Elizabethan table; vicars' board presented by nonconformists of the parish 1950; holy well in 15th cent building ¼ mile southwest.

Guide

Upton Cross has a 19th cent chapel-of-ease with apsidal chancel, nave and south porch.

LISKEARD   D. St Martin

Present church—second largest in county, with chancel, nave, north and south aisles, extra south aisle, porches, south one with parvise, west tower of three stages. North aisle has three stone-ceiled projections on north wall, chapels and porch. A Norman church, of which the font remains, and in the modern (1902) tower other relics, arch, windows, etc from the previous partly Norman tower. The rest of the building is now mostly 15th cent. Restored at various periods and later enriched.

NOTE: Norman font in north porch; arches and windows in tower; small window in west wall of north aisle; stoup in porch; roodloft stairs; piscinas; consecration crosses on exterior, unique in the county; corbel stones from previous tower under parapet; Jacobean pulpit dated 1636; Royal Arms George II 1747; fragments of old roof timbers and bosses on aisle wall; chancel arch, rare in Cornwall; slate memorials to Thomas Johnson 1666, Mary Read 1731 (exterior); notice about ladies' pattens in south porch; sundial 1779.

Dobwalls has a chapel-of-ease erected 1839 consisting of nave, with chancel formed at east end.

LITTLE PETHERICK D. St Petroc

Present church—chancel, nave, north aisle, north chapel, porch and west tower with pyramid roof. Mainly a 14th cent building with many alterations and rebuildings. 1741 south aisle remodelled; 1750 wood tower replaced with stone, all rebuilt 1858 by William White to order of the rector, Sir Hugh Molesworth, a man of vigour with Tractarian views. An extension of the north aisle involved an additional pier of catacleuse, brought from the ruined church at Constantine in St Merryn parish, as were the tower pinnacles. Much subsequent care and enrichment, especially early this century by generosity of Athelstan Riley, patron.

NOTE: Catacleuse pillar and respond from Constantine; brass to Rev Hildebrand Barker, rector 1898–1901, in vestments, with hourglass—he was a small man—'Small was the glass and scant the sand God rest the good priest Hildebrand'; curious window by roodscreen; modern screenwork in old style; font; memorial chapel to Andalusia Riley; ancient vestments (not available for view); two bells of ring of six (not accessible) medieval; 13th cent memorial slab to priest on north side of chancel.

Guide

LOOE   East Looe   D. St Mary

Present church—chancel, with apse, nave, north aisle, vestry and porches. Erected 1882–3 on site of old chapel of which 13th cent tower remains. Portland stone and marble piers.

NOTE: Alabaster and stone reredos; stained windows; circular window in north aisle; screens; font cover; old water colours; clock 1737.

LOOE   West Looe   D. St Nicholas

Present church—chancel, nave, north aisle, western turret. In part dating from 13th cent. Secularised until 1852.

NOTE: Arcade in wood from French ship *San Josef* captured

from Napoleon; stained windows; 14th cent piscina niche; 15th cent windows on south side.

LOSTWITHIEL   D. St Bartholomew
Present church—chancel, nave, north and south aisles, lean-to giving clerestory, north and south porches, and west tower with lantern and spire. Probably not founded until 1180, and until 15th cent a chapelry to Lanlivery. No traces of Norman work. Early 13th cent lower part of tower; the windows, arcades, clerestory (rare in Cornwall) and lantern spire are 14th cent. Restored 1879. No old woodwork.
NOTE: Font late 13th cent; piers of arcades without capitals, as at Fowey, and octagonal; clerestory; great five-light east window, fine example of 14th cent tracery; alabaster fragment of St Bartholomew's martyrdom; wooden almsbox dated 1645; solid seating and civic pews 1915; piscina; brass to Tristram Curteys 1423 (ask permission to rub); memorials, especially to Kendalls; arches at tower base over one-time right-of-way; the church was garrisoned in August 1644 by Parliament troops and extensively damaged by gunpowder; a horse is said to have been 'christened' at the font; carved backs of thrones of mayor and recorder 1776; Mayor Taprell's tomb by porch; lantern cross; coffin lid; sepulchral recesses in south wall exterior.

Guide

LUDGVAN   D. St Paul Apostle
Present church—chancel, nave, north and south aisles, porch and western tower of three stages, with buttresses, all mostly 14th and 15th cent. Restored 1914. Old woodwork in roofs.
NOTE: Norman font; 13th cent window on north side of chancel; slate memorial to John South 1636; shaft of Celtic cross embedded in tower steps; memorial tablet to parents of Humphrey Davey, inventor of the safety lamp, etc; old crosses in churchyard; a former incumbent was the Cornish antiquary, Rev William Borlase, 1720–72.

LUXULYAN   D. SS Ciricus and Julitta

Present church—chancel, nave, north and south aisles, porch and west tower of three stages. A Norman church stood here and the splendid font remains, but the existing building is mostly 15th cent. A window at the west end of south aisle seems to have been re-used from 14th cent structure. Restored 1883. Some old woodwork left.

NOTE: Norman font; south aisle west window; fragments of glass in tower window; Jacobean chairs; piscina; lectern carved by Canon Rashleigh, vicar 1873-91; old woodwork in north and south aisles; panels of old wood in pulpit; great blocks of granite in tower; imposing south porch with traceried ceiling; sundial 1687; memorial in churchyard to Silvanus Trevail, an architect responsible for many 19th cent Cornish schools and public buildings; old cross.

MABE   D. St Laudus

Present church—chancel, nave, north aisle and tower 14th cent. South aisle and porch 15th cent. Largely rebuilt 1869 after being struck by lightning, and since enriched. No old woodwork.

NOTE: Carving of foliage on doorways; remains of 14th cent alabaster reredos; roodloft stairs; piscina; among the communion plate is a remarkable tazza given 1577 (not accessible to view).

ST MABYN   D. St Mabena

Present church—chancel, nave, north and south aisles, porch and west tower of three stages, unbuttressed. Only the Norman font with panelled sides attests a building of that date stood here. Now all 15th cent. Restored 1884 and since. Old woodwork left in roof.

NOTE: Norman font; catacleuse stone doorway to tower; piscina; roodloft stairs; modern parclose screens; carved figures on string courses of tower and in niches under parapet; old chest; stocks; constable's truncheon; interesting silver gilt cup among communion plate (not accessible to view); painting, 'Deposition of Christ', Bassano school; memorial clock 1950.

MADRON   D. St Maddern

Present church—chancel, nave and north aisles, porches and west tower of three stages. A late 14th and 15th cent church on site of Norman structure. North aisle granite and south Beer stone. Restored 1887. Old woodwork was discovered buried and was incorporated in screen, etc. Roof woodwork largely old, and there are some bench ends, Queen Anne furnishings and good modern woodwork.

NOTE: Font, base of present font, and old font bowl near it are Norman; bench ends; screen; pulpit; belfry screen; brass to John Clies 1623 (permission to rub only given to specialists and experts); Royal Arms 1819; slate memorials to Thomas Fleming, Thomas and Alice Cock 1631, John Maddern 1621; alabaster panel, part of old reredos; charity board; banner commemorating battle of Trafalgar; sedilia; credence table; piscina; ancient inscribed stone in church wall; sundial 1770; lychgate memorial of Boer War.

Guide

MAKER   D. St Julian

Present church—chancel, nave, north and south aisles, north transept, south transept replaced by second south aisle, porch and west tower of three stages, buttressed. There was an earlier church here, appropriated to Plympton Priory about 1121, but the Norman font was brought from St Merryn about 1845 and does not necessarily indicate that there was a church here at that period. The building is mostly 15th cent, but greatly altered and restored by J. P. St Aubyn 1873–4. The old galleries were removed, the transept replaced by a second south aisle with arcade constructed with arches from alms houses at Bere Alston to make family pew for the Edgcumbes. Good modern woodwork. The tower was a signal station used by the Admiralty in 18th and 19th cent. A signalman was murdered in it 1763. A copy of the signals shown still exists in the church. NOTE: Norman font; memorials to Edgcumbe family members; sketches of unrestored church; monument to Rev Samuel Whiddon who died while preaching; tower signal chart; saint's statue niche on west front of tower, crudely made into window; curious arches at east of arcades; projections on pier capital; interesting headstones in churchyard: one to a child who swallowed a stone—size recorded; another to John Roper with verse, 'What I was is no affair of yours'; St Julian's well, 14th cent well house, 200 yards north.

Guide

MANACCAN   D. Uncertain

Present church—chancel, nave, north aisle, south transept, porch and west tower of two stages 14th cent. Norman church, cruciform, with 13th cent alterations and 14th and 15th cent additions (north aisle and chapel). Restored 1888. Old roofs exactly reproduced at restoration, chancel chairs, pulpit, etc made from original timber.

NOTE: Norman south door, with three orders (reconstructed); lancet windows in chancel and transept; stoup; piscina in south transept; roodloft stairs; Norman corbel head over arch of south door; traces of squint at chancel transept angle, as at Landewednack, etc; fig tree growing out of south wall of tower.

Guide

MARAZION   D. All Saints

Present church—chancel with apse, nave, north and south aisles, vestry, porch and gable turret. Chapel of St Hermes, medieval, became ruinous and was rebuilt 1735. Present church built 1861. Architect J. P. St Aubyn.

NOTE: Memorial windows, one to J. P. St Aubyn, 1895.

MARHAMCHURCH D. St Marwenne

Present church—chancel, nave, north aisle, south transept, porch and west tower of three stages, with buttresses. Very possibly a small Norman church here. Now mainly 15th cent. Restored 1907. Old woodwork remains in roofs.

NOTE: Cresset stone; curious stone window, remains of anchorite's cell 1403; Royal Arms Charles II; old roofs; old ironwork on south door 15th cent; piscina; aumbry; Jacobean pulpit; bench end in chancel; 17th cent slate memorials; memorial window to John Kingdon 1843, rector for 50 years; statue of St Marwenne; Victorian cross brass c 1840.

Guide

ST MARTIN-BY-LOOE
D. St Martin

Present church—chancel, nave, south aisle, south and north transepts, porch and west tower. Traces of Norman building; the north door, not helped by a modern porch, is of that date, as are parts of the font. There is a 13th cent window in corner of west wall of south aisle, and blocked west door of tower is also of this date. Later cents added north transept, south transept, 15th cent south aisle. Lower parts of tower 13th and 14th cent. Restored 1882 and 1907. Some old woodwork in roofs and screens. Good modern woodwork.

NOTE: Norman north door and parts of font; small 13th cent window near organ; blocked door of tower; piscina; coffin-stone of priest c 1300; parclose screens dated 1612; memorial with effigies to Walter Langdon 1677; slate memorial to Philip Mayow 1590; Elizabethan altar table in chapel; good modern pews and font cover; model of Looe drifter; sundial on south transept gable; a rector here, Rev Jonathan Toup 1750–85, was famous in European learned circles.

Guide

Page 117
(left) Bench-end,
St Winnow,
sixteenth century;
(right) pulpit, St Mary
Magdalene, Launceston,
mid-sixteenth century

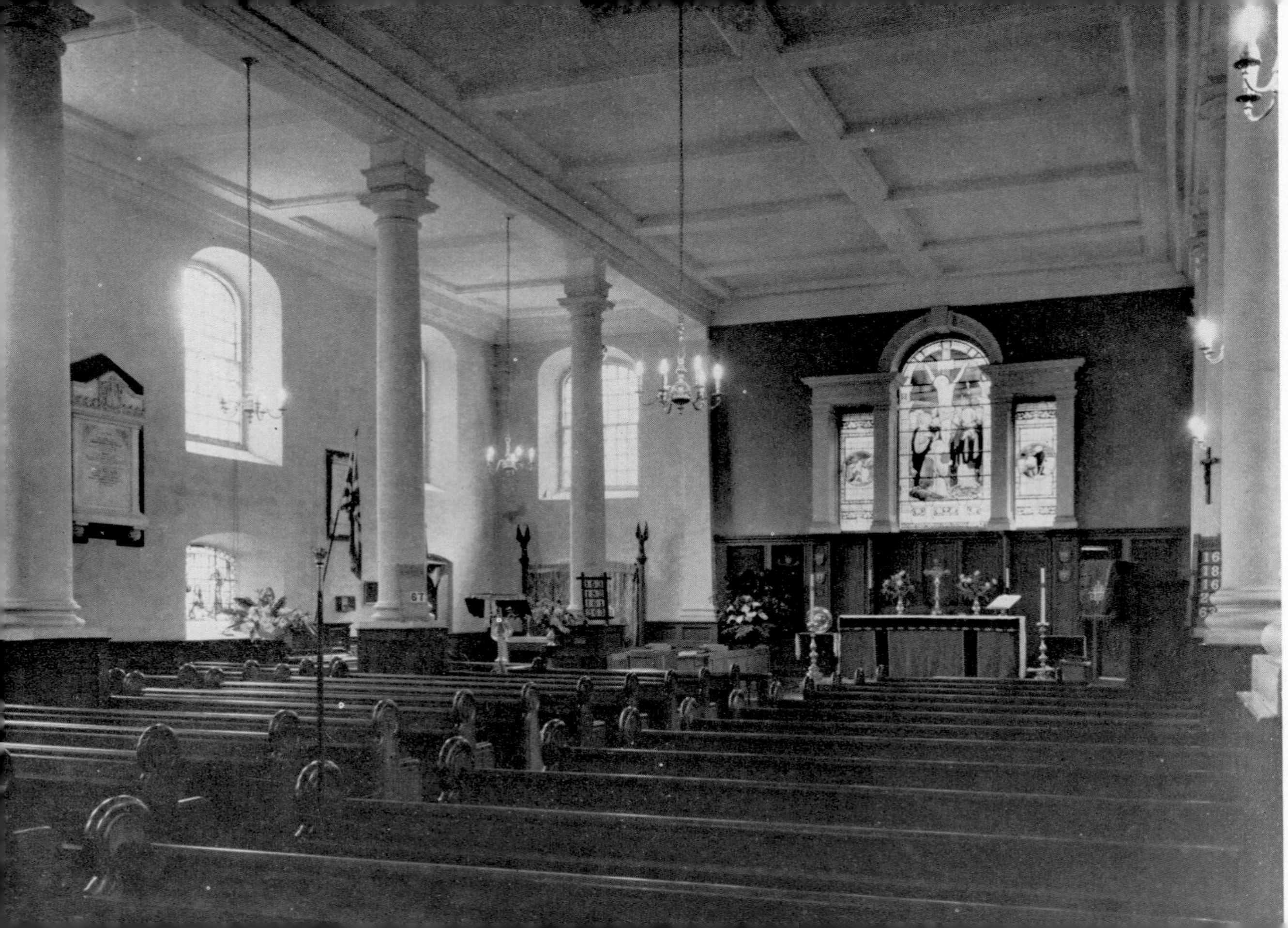

Page 118 *St Euny, Redruth, 1756*

ST MARTIN-IN-MENEAGE
D. St Martin
Present church—a plain rectangular building erected in 1830 with the 15th cent tower of an older building, of which no trace remains.

MARYFIELD See under Antony

ST MAWGAN-IN-MENEAGE
D. St Mawgan
Present church—chancel, nave, north aisle, north and south transepts, porch and western tower of three stages. There are traces here of a 13th cent structure, with 15th cent tower and north aisle. Restored 1894 by Edmund Sedding. Old woodwork remains in the roofs. The squint at the junction of the south transept and chancel is of the same plan as those at Cury and Landewednack, but of better detail in the columns, arches and window. The minor shafts of the font are curved around the shape of the bowl in a peculiar manner.

NOTE: Curious font; squint and arches in transept/chancel; roodloft stairs; lancet windows 13th cent; effigies of Robert Carminow and wife; stoup in porch; sword and helmet of Sir Richard Vyvyan, Royalist in Civil War; small brass inscription to Hannibal Baffer 1708 (ask permission to rub); tower pinnacles of clustered shafts; carved figure on keystone of tower west window; shields on arch of door; carved jambs of same door; carved jambs to north aisle east window; sundial 1695.

MAWGAN-IN-PYDAR
D. St Mawgan and St Nicholas
Present church—chancel, nave, north transept, south aisle, porch and tower on south side, with stair turret and spirelet. Originally a cruciform 13th cent church, with tower at south transept. 14th cent chapel to chancel, south aisle and upper part of tower added 15th cent. Restored 1861 by W. Butterfield.

MAWNAN

Old woodwork in screen, pulpit and bench ends. Modern parclose and belfry screens.

NOTE: Font c 1430; Marian pulpit 1553; interesting 15th cent screen; about 40 bench ends; brasses to priest 1420 and to members of the Arundell family 1570–80 (ask permission to rub); modern brass tablets; slate memorials to Henry and Dorothy Stephen 1630; good modern windows; old iron crucifix over pulpit; 16th cent statue of St Nicholas; 14th cent catacleuse stone arches in south aisle of chancel; hatchment c 1820; slate altar stone restored to position; old crosses in churchyard; boat stem memorial 1846; proximity of manor house, home of the Arundells, now a convent; medieval bell c 1410 in tower.

Guide

MAWNAN   D. St Maunan and Stephen
Present church—chancel, nave, north and south aisles, porch and west tower of two stages 14th cent. Slight traces of 13th cent work in chancel, the rest except tower is 15th cent. Nave roof restored 1684. Church restored 1880.

NOTE: Part of screen with painted panels; 17th cent almsbox; piscina; 13th cent stone coffin lid with engraved cross; 13th cent lancet window in chancel; roodloft stairs; carved head at end of north aisle; modern embroidery; ancient earthwork surrounding church; cross head built into outside wall; holy well with arched chamber.

Guide

ST MELLION   D. St Melanius
Present church—chancel, nave, north aisle, south transept, porch and west tower of three stages. Norman church stood here, and the lower parts of the nave, chancel and transept walls are of that period. In the 15th cent the north aisle and arcade and porch were added with the tower. Restored 1862.

Old woodwork in nave and aisle roofs. Bishop Bronescombe
dedicated the previous church here 1259.
NOTE: Brass to Peter Coryton and 24 children 1551 (ask permission to rub); ancient helmet and spur; imposing memorials
to Corytons of 17th, 18th and 20th cents; modern statue of St
Melanius; piscinas in chancel and transept; Jacobean pulpit.

MENHENIOT D. St Lalluwy, St Antoninus
Present church—chancel, nave, north and south aisles, porches
and west tower with spire. No earlier remains discernible.
Mostly 15th cent. Restored 1925 by G. Fellowes Prynne.
NOTE: Font; inscribed brass to Ralph Carmynhow 1386 (ask
permission to rub); memorials; representation of ship on
memorial to Vice-Admiral Charles Trelawny 1891; lectern
with figure of William of Wykeham, sometime rector; modern
and Victorian woodwork; sedilia and piscina.

ST MERRYN   D. St Merryn
Present church—chancel, nave, south aisle, north transept
porch and west tower of three stages. Norman cruciform
church stood here. Font now at Maker. 13th cent transept, 15th
cent south aisle. Restored 1887–1907 and again 1962. A little
old recovered woodwork is worked into modern seating.
NOTE: 15th cent catacleuse stone font from Constantine, a
ruined church in the sands (the catacleuse quarry was in this
parish and much used from the late 14th cent, though known
earlier) 15th cent catacleuse arcade; stocks; stoups; 17th cent
stone memorial; corbels from Constantine in churchyard wall;
ringers' rules; Royal Arms Charles II.
Guide

MERTHER See under Tresillian

MEVAGISSEY   D. St Peter
              (SS Meva and Issey)
Present church—chancel, nave, north aisle, south transept,

porch. Traces of cruciform building of Norman date, including Norman font. The rest is mainly 15th cent. Only the tower base is ancient. Restored by J. P. St Aubyn 1887–8, who put saddle-back roof on tower.

NOTE: Norman font; 14th cent window in transept; slate memorial to Lewis Dart 1632; memorial in chancel to Otwell and Mary Hill 17th cent; Royal Arms; tower base: the tower became ruinous during the Commonwealth, the bells were sold to a St Austell Quaker, one Grouden, to raise funds for taking the tower down. Hence the local rhyme (the popular name for the harbour town once being Porthilly):

> Ye men of Porthilly
> Why were ye so silly
> In having so little a power?
> You sold every bell
> As Gorran men tell
> For money to pull down your tower.

ST MEWAN   D. St Mewan

Present church—chancel, nave, south aisle and short north aisle, porch and west tower. Mostly 15th cent, but Norman remains in north wall and lower part of font. There is a 13th cent piscina in chancel respond, the south aisle and priest's doorway are 15th cent. The tower top became ruinous and the stones belonging to it are said to be at a nearby farm; local legend says the devil took them away. The tower remains at two stages since the Commonwealth. Restored harshly 1865. No old woodwork left.

NOTE: Font base; 15th cent door; piscina; stunted tower; modern woodwork; clock in vestry with case a model of tower; good memorial on wall to Sir Francis Layland-Barrett 1933.

ST MICHAEL CAERHAYES
D. St Michael

Present church—chancel, nave, north transept, south aisle or chapel, porch and tower at west end of three stages, built without buttresses.

There was a cruciform Norman church here of which the font and north doorway remain. A short south aisle of 15th cent date and a 14th or early 15th cent tower have been added to the remodelled earlier church. Restored 1864. Some of the woodwork and some windows are the work of Rev William Willimott, rector 1852–78 (see Quethiock).

NOTE: Norman font and north doorway with simple Agnus Dei tympanum; armour and weapons said to have been used at Bosworth Field 1485; part 13th cent tomb in transept wall; piscina in chancel; carved screen and windows by Rev William Willimott; effigy of Trafalgar seaman; roodloft stairs; stoup in porch; two medieval bells in ring of six; new buttress to tower (1970) enables bells to be rung after many years' silence.

Guide

ST MICHAEL PENKEVIL
D. St Michael

Present church—13th cent chancel and nave, 14th cent transepts and tower. For a period (1319–1426) this was a collegiate church with four altars, one in tower, the base of which remains though the mensa has been removed. Rebuilt and restored by G. E. Street in 1862 using old material recut.

NOTE: Consecration stone of 1261; altar in tower; fragments of old worked stone; coffin lids 13th cent; brasses to John Trenowyth 1497, John Trembras, priest, 1515, and others of 17th cent (ask permission to rub); many memorials to Boscawens of Tregothnan; sedilia; piscinas; niches; recesses for valuables in transepts; lectern carved by Belgian refugees.

MICHAELSTOW   D. St Michael

Present church—chancel, south chancel aisle, nave, north and south aisles, porch and west tower of three stages. Normans erected a church here of which there are traces at the east end.

But the church is mostly 15th cent with some evidence of 13th cent structure. There is a 13th cent piscina on the outside of the north chancel wall and a quatrefoil window (blocked) in the same wall inside, which are supposed to indicate the presence of an anchorite's cell in that century. Restored 1869, but much old woodwork remains with benches, roofs, etc.

NOTE: 15th cent font; anchorite's squint (?); good 15th and 16th cent benches and bench ends; Royal Arms 1727; one of the bells is medieval; slate memorial to Jane Merifield 1662; sundial 1684; tall ancient cross in churchyard; 'holy well'.

MILLBROOK   D. All Saints
Present church—chancel, nave, north and south aisles, porch and base of tower built 1895. 15th cent style church of some dignity. Polyphant piers in arcades, barrel roofs.

NOTE: Modern stained windows; nave roof excellent example of late-Victorian work.

MINSTER   D. St Materiana
Present church—chancel, nave, remodelled 13th cent west tower, 15th cent south aisle and porch. Originally a priory. A Norman church existed here, of which font and other evidences remain. In 1870 more or less ruinous and drastic restoration was necessary; J. P. St Aubyn architect. All old woodwork destroyed, including good screen.

NOTE: Norman font; small 13th cent window in chancel; slate memorials to John Hender 1611, William and Elizabeth Cotton 1656; brass to Hender Roberts 1602 (ask permission to rub); Jacobean table; fragments of heraldic glass 16th cent; scissor-like carving on west wall of tower.

ST MINVER   D. St Menefreda
Present church—chancel, nave, north and south aisles, porch, and west tower with spire. Late-Norman traces in north arcade and north chancel wall. South aisle and tower are 15th cent. Restored 1873 by J. P. St Aubyn, tower and spire rebuilt

1875. Some old woodwork in fine bench ends and belfry screen (part of roodscreen), roofs and panels.
NOTE: North arcade; bench ends and belfry screen; leaning spire; brass of Roger Opy 1517 (ask permission to rub); slate memorial to Elizabeth and Thomas Stone 1586, 1604; John Silly 1672; good modern woodwork; relics of previous church at back of nave; Queen Anne communion rails; roodloft stairs; pillar piscina; consecration cross on right of porch doorway; sundial; Royal Arms Charles II 1660; stocks.

There are two ancient chapels or daughter-churches:
St Enodoc is a Norman cruciform church of which much remains, and 15th cent south chancel chapel; tower at north transept as at Blisland with 13th cent spire. Restored 1873 by J. P. St Aubyn.
NOTE: Norman font; part of screen; tower and spire; stoup of catacleuse, now an almsbox; bell recovered from wreck; slate memorial in churchyard to John and Alice Mably 1687; piscina; this church roofless in 1860 and largely buried in sand.

Rock, Porthilly (D. St Michael)
Present church—chancel, nave, south chancel aisle, south transept, north vestry on site of transept, porch base of tower with saddle-back roof. A Norman chapel, of which the font remains. South transept enlarged in 13th and 15th cent. Restored 1865 by J. P. St Aubyn.
NOTE: Norman font; piscinas; Tudor pulpit; part of screen; slate memorial to William Rounsevall 1659; roodloft stairs.

MITHIAN   D. St Peter
Present church—chancel, nave, transepts, south porch and west tower. Erected 1861 by William White, architect. There was formerly a spire, taken down 1898, and a new three-stage tower was erected in 1928. It is used as a trigonometrical station.
NOTE: Interior proportions; roodscreen.

Guide

MORVAH   D. St Bridget of Sweden
Present church—plain square building erected 1828, attached
to 14th cent two-stage tower of earlier church.
NOTE: Tower; Swedish flag; glass candlesticks and other ornaments of Swedish manufacture.

MORVAL   D. St Wenna
Present church—chancel, nave, north aisle, south transept,
porch and west tower of three stages, mainly 15th cent. Old
woodwork in north aisle roof. The windows in this aisle are
high in the wall owing to the lie of the ground outside. Harshly
restored.
NOTE: Tower arch springing from corbels; Royal Arms (from
gallery front?); slate memorial to Walter Coode 1637; hat pegs
along wall; Victorian texts on tin panels; sundial 1671; initials
'I B 1671' over transept door, a private pew of Buller family.

MORWENSTOW   D. St John Baptist
Present church—chancel, nave, north and south aisles, porch
and west tower of three stages. Norman church with at least a
north aisle, which survives; 15th cent tower, south aisle 15th
cent Polyphant and granite in arcade, porch reconstructed with
Norman doorway and one order or arch ring on outer wall. Old
woodwork remains in roofs, fine bench ends and a few bits in the
screen.
NOTE: Pre-Norman font; Norman doorway, piers, arches and
beak heads, etc dissimilar design; date 1564 (sometimes read as
1664) on south aisle capital; next has 'This is the house of the
Lord' (upside down?); portion of ancient wall painting (St
Morwenna); screen, possibly with bits of old woodwork from
one erected 1575; Jacobean chair and table; memorial windows;
slate memorial to John Kempthorne 1591; carved symbolic
panel; 'Parson Hawker' was vicar here 1834–75, poet, writer,
character, idealist and exhibitionist; churchyard memorials to
shipwrecked sailors; no belfry window on west face of tower.

Guide

MOUNT HAWKE D. St John Baptist

Present church—chancel, and nave with south porch. Erected
1878. Architect Charles Hancock. The font is said to be Norman,
worked over and denuded of any ornament.

NOTE: Font, possibly from Trevaunance manor chapel, St
Agnes, recut; bishop's chair presented by Kensington School of
Mines, who use a local mine for study purposes.

MULLION   D. St Melanius

Present church—chancel, nave, north and south aisles, porch
and (1512) west tower of two stages, serpentine blocks used with
granite as in other Meneage churches. Traces of 14th cent
church on site of earlier building but mostly now late 15th cent.
Restored with care 1878–83. Much outstanding old woodwork,
benches, bench ends, roofs and part screen.

NOTE: Numerous fine benches and bench ends; Royal Arms
Charles II; brass to Thomas Flavel, dispossessed rector under
Commonwealth, restored 1660 (ask permission to rub); odd
openings at roodscreen in arcades; carving of crucifixion on
west wall of tower; Elizabethan carved figures on lectern;
panelled jambs of porch; stoup; dog's door in south door,
original woodwork.

MYLOR   D. St Melorus

Present church—chancel, nave, south aisle, north and south
transepts, porch, gable turret and detached low bell tower.
Norman building on water's edge, of which north transept,
north nave wall and doorway, north chancel walls and some
stones in west doorway are original. 15th cent south aisle and
porch. Restored 1869–70, including new south transept. Some
old woodwork remains. Church repaved with old slate headstones.

NOTE: Norman north doorway and west doorway with tympanum; 15th cent pillar piscina; south porch with panelled
jambs and tracery; hatchments; 16th cent pulpit; Royal Arms
Charles I and Anne; part of ancient screen; 13th cent panel of

crucifixion on outer wall; largest old cross in Cornwall in churchyard; memorials to prominent Cornishmen, especially sea captains; oak screen memorial to *Darlwyne* victims 1966; sundial memorial to novelist Howard Spring 1966.

Guide

ST NECTAN or ST NIGHTON See under St Winnow

ST NEOT   D. St Anietus

Present church—chancel, nave, north and south aisles, porch with parvise and pinnacles, and west tower of three stages, buttressed. The embattled south aisle is 15th cent, as is tower. The north aisle is early 16th cent, windows without hood moulding. The porch ceiling is groined. The church is justly famed for the range of windows of 16th cent date. These have been carefully restored, even in the unlikely early 19th cent (1826) and since. They are memorials to the generosity of the whole parish before the religious unity of the community was broken. They reflect the late-medieval confusion of the Celtic saint, Anietus, with the better known St Neot.

NOTE: Font, date doubtful; ranges of splendid windows; groining of porch roof and parvise; recess—Easter Sepulchre?—on north side of sanctuary; modern screen; organ by Willis; embattled south aisle; lantern cross in churchyard; slate memorial, table tomb, to William Bere 1610: 'Here lyeth Bere whom Angelles to heaven beare'; oak tree branch displayed from the tower to commemorate the escape of Charles II after the battle of Worcester, renewed every year; sundial on south wall. Modern village co-operation in 1970s raised large sums to restore this church.

Guide

ST NEWLYN EAST D. St Newlina

Present church—chancel with south aisle, nave, south aisle and south transept, north transept, porch and west tower of three stages. Norman church was cruciform. The north transept lower walls and font remain, though the minor shafts of the latter have been replaced with serpentine marble. Enlarged in 13th and 14th cent; south aisle, south transept, porch and tower are 15th cent. Restored 1883 by J. D. Sedding. Old woodwork in bench ends, parclose screen and south aisle roof. Good modern woodwork incorporates some old pieces. Enriched at various times.

NOTE: Norman font; lantern cross head 15th cent; bench ends; piscinas in south transept and double piscina late 13th or 14th cent in chancel aisle (vestry); 13th cent lancet in north transept; roodloft stairs, now entrance to pulpit; 17th cent helmet, supposedly that of Sir John Arundell, who held Pendennis Castle for the king in 1646; screens; old chairs; Royal Arms Charles I; memorials to members of Arundell family of Trerice, one with bust 1691; modern woodwork; niche over doorway; sundial 19th cent; large fig tree growing from outside wall, supposed to be cursed—anyone plucking leaves will die within a twelve-month.

Guide

NEWLYN D. St Peter

Present church—chancel, nave, north and south aisles, transepts and porch in 14th cent style erected 1865–6. North aisle added 1888. Restored by Martin Travers in 1920 and enriched in time of Rev A. G. Wyon, vicar 1936–55 and well known artist.

NOTE: Memorial windows 19th cent; statue of Virgin and Child by Wyon and crucifix carved by him; painting of 'The Entombment' by Ernest Procter, ARA; Italian tabernacle; noteworthy church garden with rare plants (no cuttings please).

St Andrew's chapel-of-ease is open only on Wednesdays; has another Wyon crucifix and two modern works by local artists: a tryptych, 'Creation', and a tapestry, 'Descent of the Spirit'.

NEWQUAY   D. St Michael

Present church—chancel, nave, north and south aisles, porches, the south one with parvise, and tower of three stages at south-west corner. Modern church 1911 on grand scale in Cornish style by Sir Ninian Comper. Richly furnished. Tower 1968 is not successful in reproducing characteristic Cornish appearance. NOTE: Font, the gift of Dr E. B. Pusey; font cover; lectern; screen; fine organ and case in 18th cent style 1961; Polyphant arcades; stained windows; new tower.

Guide

NORTH HILL   D. St Torney

Present church—chancel, nave, north and south aisles, groined porch with parvise and stately west tower of three stages. The whole church is a spacious and interesting building reflecting past local prosperity. Mostly 15th cent; the south or Tre-bartha aisle, with buttressed and ornamented parapet, is late 15th or early 16th cent; the chancel, in rubble contrasting with the granite, is earlier, 14th cent. The porch, with parvise above, has a groined ceiling. Old roofs remain, but no other old woodwork.
NOTE: Roodloft stairs in north wall built up; half columns on north wall and north arcade above roodscreen level, purpose unknown; niches for statues and 'Easter Sepulchre' in chancel; old communion table at back; old three-lock chest dated 1750; Spoure monument 17th cent, inlaid heraldic device on their pew; slate memorial to Vincent family 1606; Royal Arms Charles II; good benches and bench ends 1897; mural tablet (in Rodd pew) to child in a chrysom garment, found in chapel of Trebartha Hall; sundial 1753.

NORTH PETHERWIN
D. St Paternus

Present church—chancel, nave with clerestory, north chancel aisle, north and south aisles, porches and west tower of three stages. Norman piers on north side with reconstructed arches and base of font show a church of some dignity stood here at that period. 14th and 16th cent additions on the north side and a south aisle in the 15th cent with graceful piers, a 14th cent tower comprise the church at present. Restored 1876. Some old woodwork in roofs, screen, altar rails (now at back). Good modern woodwork.

NOTE: Norman piers and base to font; junction of north nave arcade and north chancel chapel, clever adaption; 16th cent ironwork on south door; Jacobean communion rails 1685 at belfry arch; old roofs in chancel, porch and south aisle; screens; old fragments of stone in vestry; modern woodwork; slate memorials to Dorothy Killigrew 1634, Ann Yeo 1638.

Guide

NORTH TAMERTON
D. St Denys or Dionysius (?)
Present church—largely 15th cent chancel, nave, south aisle, porch and fine west tower of three stages, with carved band round base. Possibly once a Norman nave and chancel church. Restored 1875. Some good old bench ends.

NOTE: Norman (?) font; numerous excellent bench ends; brass to Leonard Loveis 1576 (ask permission to rub); piscina in south aisle; tiled wall to sanctuary; 18th cent chest; 17th cent chair; carvings on chancel stalls (monkeys?); Rev John Wesley preached here in the 1740s.

OTTERHAM   D. St Denis
Present church—chancel, nave, south aisle, porch and west tower. A featureless church drastically restored 1889–90. Before 1850 there was a small north transept; the north wall is largely a windowless blank since its removal. No old woodwork left.

NOTE: Old font base, possibly Norman; two old font bowls; piscina; slate memorial to Mary French 1652; two medieval bells (inaccessible) 15th cent, and one other, all chimed by churchwarden, one in each hand and the other with his foot.

PADSTOW   D. St Petroc

Present church—chancel, nave, north and south aisles, porch and west tower of three stages. St Petroc, 'Prince of the saints of Cornwall', established his first monastery here. Of the earlier churches undoubtedly on this site only two broken fragments of stone crosses remain. There is possibly Norman masonry in the lowest stage of the tower. The 14th cent south aisle slightly earlier than the north aisle. The rest mainly 15th cent. Woodwork in roofs and fine carved bosses of same period. The parish long enjoyed the right of sanctuary.

NOTE: 15th cent bench end of fox in priest's vestments preaching to geese; carved figure over piscina in chancel; flamboyant tracery in south aisle windows; 16th cent pulpit; brass to Lawrence Merther, vicar 1400–21 (ask permission to rub); monument to Humphrey Prideaux 1627; organ by Telford, built in Dublin, brought here by sea; catacleuse stone font; ring of six bells; a half-muffled peal is rung here every August in fulfilment of the will of Nicholas Watts 1632; headstone of Caleb Boney, versatile Cornish mechanician and musician in churchyard.

Guide

Trevone, a recent chapel-of-ease with excellent use of traditional Cornish material. Gallery with organ at back, shaped around circular west window.

PAR (Biscovey)   D. St Mary

Present church—chancel, wide nave, south chapel, porch in base of tower with spire on south-west corner of church. Erected 1849, the first complete church by G. E. Street. The tower a much simplified copy of Lostwithiel, which Street much admired. The first incumbent of this parish was Rev George Rundle Prynne, hymnwriter and afterwards the much-persecuted vicar of St Peter's, Plymouth, whose courageous ministry in the Plymouth cholera epidemic dissipated all opposition to his 'ritualism'.

NOTE: Odd window in sedilia by altar; timber roof trusses; dissimilar pillars in south chapel; inscribed cross-shaft in churchyard.

Good Shepherd is a chapel-of-ease by Edmund Sedding 1896, with modern cloister passage to Gott Memorial Hall.

PAUL   D. St Pol de Leon
Present church—15th and 16th cent chancel, nave, north and south aisles, porch and west tower of three stages. The church was burnt in 1595 by a Spanish force landed nearby. Restoration 1892–3. No old woodwork remains and there has been rebuilding.
NOTE: Traces of fire in north arcade piers; box pews; small arch between nave and aisles; recently discovered piscina; wooden panels with texts 1716; semi-circular communion rail; helmet and armour of William Godolphin 1689; 18th cent memorial in Cornish to Stephen Hutchins; good east window; chandelier; sundial; monument in churchyard wall to Dolly Pentreath, said (incorrectly) to be the last to speak the Cornish language in 1778; cross in same wall; niches at sides of west window in tower.

PELYNT   D. St Nonna
Present church—chancel, nave, short north aisle, south vestry and transept (Trelawny aisle), porch and west tower of three stages. No traces of Norman building. The tower may be 14th cent and the remainder 15th cent, but all has been remodelled. The north arcade of Tuscan columns is probably late 17th cent and the restoration in 1882–3 was harsh, leaving shiny tiles as a dado along the walls. No old woodwork survives except carved bosses of roofs, and possibly other woodwork hidden beneath ceiling plaster.
NOTE: Tuscan arcade; Bishop Trelawny's chair and staff 1721; tomb chest in sanctuary, Francis Buller 1616; other slate memorials to William Achym 1589, Edward Trelawny 1630,

PENCOYS

Cordelia Trelawny 1634, and Elizabeth Pope 1654; helmet and gauntlets in transept; windows in nave roof unusual; memorial tablet to six sons of Rev W. S. Grigson, former vicar.

PENCOYS   D. St Andrew

Present church—chancel and nave 1881 in lancet style.

NOTE: Stained east window; interesting connection with work of Rev W. Broadley of Carnmenellis and his widow 'Mother Maria Charlotte', who gave toward the endowment £2,300 from her small means. (See Carnmenellis.)

PENDEEN   D. St John Baptist

Present church—cruciform, chancel, nave, communicants' area, transepts, south porch and west tower. All erected 1851. Designed by Rev Robert Aitken, powerful and resourceful evangelist, and built by the miners under his direction and inspiration.

NOTE: Aitken's symbolic memorial in chancel; roundels of Flemish glass in windows; stained glass in east window made by unique process; castellated surrounding wall.

Guide

PENPONDS   D. Holy Trinity

Present church—chancel, nave, north aisle, south porch. Erected 1844. Restored 1901, and enriched with good modern woodwork.

NOTE: Good ample modern woodwork 1901 with some old panels; good stained glass.

PENWERRIS   D. St Michael

Erected 1827, a square box with pepper pot adornment, castellations on the east front—the nadir of ecclesiastical architecture before the Cambridge Camden Society and the Ecclesiological Society got to work. Successive attempts have been made to make it worshipful. Made parochial 1848.

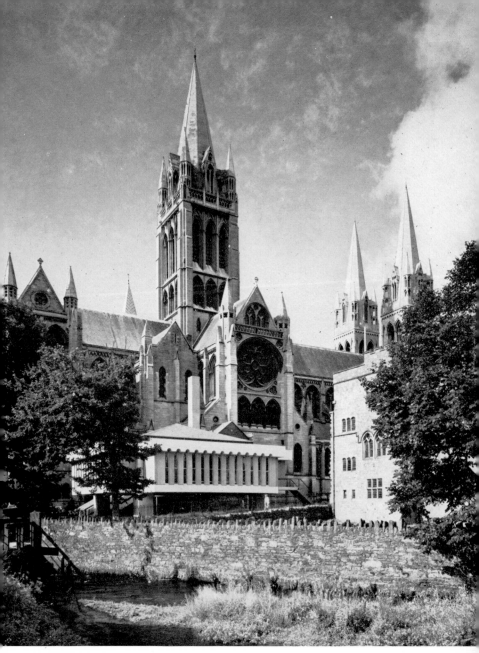

Page 135   *The Cathedral, Truro, 1880–1910, with Chapter House, 1967*

Page 136 (above) *Carbis Bay, twentieth-century traditional;* (below) *St Day, twentieth-century contemporary*

NOTE: West gallery; memorials; general shape, proportion and adornment of building.

PENZANCE   D. St John Baptist

Present church—chancel, nave, north and south transepts, lean-to aisles and porches. Erected 1881 in 13th cent style.

NOTE: Screen of metalwork; reredos, a tryptych depicting the Annunciation, the Nativity and Christ as the Tree of Life; memorials; good stained windows; lectern.

PENZANCE   D. St Mary-the-Virgin

Present church—quasi-chancel, nave, north and south aisles, galleries, west vestibule and grand west tower of three stages. An ancient spired chapel stood here on the bold headland which gives the town its name. In 1834 this chapel was replaced by the present boldly-conceived structure by Charles Hutchins. The interior has been improved by decoration and removal of surplus pews. Made parochial 1871.

NOTE: Altarpiece by Ernest Procter; local scene and skyline; pillar almsbox dated 1612 from old chapel; representation of head of St John Baptist on a charger; ancient cross in church-yard; top part of spire of old steeple; fine modern crucifix.

PENZANCE   D. St Paul

Present church—chancel, nave, transepts, north aisle; west porch, in lancet style, of 13th cent derivation. Erected 1843 as a Tractarian foundation at his own cost of £5,000 by Rev Henry Batten, curate-in-charge. The first midnight communion in Cornwall held here Christmas 1857.

NOTE: Granite pulpit; old chair; stained glass by Willement.

PERRANARWORTHAL
D. St Piran

Present church—chancel, nave, south aisle, porch and west tower of three stages. Once a Norman church stood here but

I

all, apart from the 15th cent tower, was rebuilt 1882 by J. P. St Aubyn. No old woodwork remains.

NOTE: Part of Norman tympanum; stained windows.

Guide

PERRANUTHNOE   D. St Piran

Present church—chancel, nave, north aisle, south transept, porch and west tower of three stages. An earlier church gave way to this mostly 15th cent building with traces of 13th and 14th cent work. Practically rebuilt 1883, except tower. No old woodwork left, good modern screenwork, etc.

NOTE: Norman font, square, with panelled sides; roodloft stairs; squint from transept; carved keystone of south doorway; small statue of St James from destroyed chapel at Goldsithney (?).

PERRANZABULOE   D. St Piran

Present church—chancel, nave, south aisle, transepts, porch and west tower. This is the third church of this parish, and was erected 1804 with the materials from the previous 12th cent church which had 14th and 15th cent additions. In the removal to its present position the tower was shortened and other alterations made. The present church was restored in 1873 and later enriched with modern woodwork. The previous church, whose site is still visible near the sand dunes near the beach, was itself preceded by the earliest, which is the Oratory of St Piran, dating possibly from the time of that saint himself (6th cent) or from the period immediately following his death. The Oratory, 29ft by 16½ft externally, was uncovered in a storm in 1835, in a more complete form than it shows at present. The protecting building was erected in 1909–10 but the whole may have to be buried again for protection against water and vandalism.

NOTE: The present church—font; bench ends in pulpit; slate memorial to Perran and Elizabeth Hoskyn 1675.

The second church site—ancient cross.

The Oratory—unmortared walls; doorway; altar.

PHILLACK   D. St Felicitas (St Piala)

Present church—chancel, nave, north and south aisles, porch
and west tower of three stages. The district was a very early
Christian settlement. Here a Norman cruciform church was
eventually built, enlarged 15th cent and rebuilt 1856. Some
fragments of old woodwork remain.

NOTE: Chi-Rho stone 5th cent and early crucifix in porch;
part-Norman capital in wall; font; altar slab; sedilia; piscina;
corbel heads; stone coffin lid; tomb slab; memorials to Hockin
family, several members of whom served as rectors for long
periods.

PHILLEIGH   D. St Filius

Present church—chancel, nave, south aisle, north transept,
porch and west 13th cent tower of two stages. 13th–15th cent
building, rebuilt 1867, possibly under direction of Rev C. W.
Carlyon, architect-rector of St Just-in-Roseland. No old
woodwork.

NOTE: 13th cent font; piscina in chancel respond; Royal Arms;
monuments 1680, etc; good proportion of arcade.

PILLATON   D. St Odulph

Present church—chancel, nave, north aisle, south transept,
porch and west tower of three stages. No trace of earlier building although one dedicated here in 1259. All 15th cent.
Restored 1878. Old woodwork remains in north aisle and
transept.

NOTE: Two ancient piscinas; squint and roodloft stairs through
passage from transept to chancel (cf Quethiock); aumbry in
transept; recess in north aisle; memorials; stained windows to
former rectors; Royal Arms Charles II 1663; stocks.

ST PINNOCK   D. St Pynnocus

Present church—chancel, nave, north aisle, south transept,
porch and west tower of three stages. Possibly once cruciform,

but now mostly 15th cent and remodelled. Heavily restored 1882. Old woodwork remains in the porch only.
NOTE: Font; roof of porch; lychgate; ancient cross in church-yard; 17th cent memorials.

PORT ISAAC   D. St Peter

Present church—chancel and nave of 1882, with lancet windows and porch.
NOTE: Memorial organ 1939–45.

PORTHLEVEN   D. St Bartholomew

1842 church, remodelled 1893 by G. Fellowes Prynne in Romanesque style with apsidal sanctuary, nave and baptistry. Lady chapel built 1934 by C. R. Corfield. Vestry 1962.
NOTE: Good modern carved woodwork; stained windows.

POUGHILL   D. St Olaf

Present church—chancel, nave, north and south aisles, porch and west tower of three stages. Possibly first a cruciform church. A north aisle with 14th cent Caen stone arcade and eastern bay of south aisle. In 15th cent a granite arcade completed the south aisle. Much old woodwork remains in roof and seats.
NOTE: Norman font in belfry; splendid bench ends and seats; 13th cent piscina in sanctuary; 15th cent wall paintings of St Christopher; slate memorial to Laurence Braginton, vicar, 1739; officiant's desk facing people, a survival; niche over porch door; old communion table; oak gates to belfry; Royal Arms Charles II; pulpit 1880, carved by a parishioner; Sir Goldsworthy Gurney tablet; slate plaque in porch commemorates stay during war of Clifton College, Bristol; in churchyard old font basin; the parish possesses the oldest registers (1537) in the diocese.

Guide

POUNDSTOCK   D. St Neot (?)

Present church—chancel, nave, north aisle, south transept, tower at west end, mostly 14th and 15th cent. Carefully restored 1896. Old woodwork in roofs, seats and part screen. NOTE: Font; fragments of Norman building; one odd pier in chancel; Trebarfoote memorial 1630; Penfound memorial in north aisle chapel; painted panels of roodscreen; old woodwork in choir stalls; modern ornaments and statues, some also antique; fragments of ancient glass; slate memorial to Trebarfoote family; wall painting of Christ of the Trades, carefully and expertly restored; guild house in churchyard.

Guide

PROBUS   D. SS Probus and Grace

Present church—chancel, nave, north and south aisles, porches. West tower the highest in Cornwall and justly famed for its grandeur and detail. In Celtic days a monastic foundation. Later a collegiate church with a dean and five canons. Normans built a church here, of which the piscina in southeast of sanctuary is a reminder. Now largely a stately 15th cent church. Tower was begun just before 1523, the parishioners doing the labouring. A dispute over ownership of the quarry delayed building and it was probably not finished until the reign of Mary. Extensive restoration by G. E. Street 1851. Later restorations and enrichments. South choir aisle 1904 a good copy; the east window and Hawkins memorial were moved from the old walls. NOTE: Piscina in south aisle (where it ended prior to 1904); old base of screen 1591 with punning motto; brass to John and Cecilia Wolvedon in south aisle 1514 (ask permission to rub); screen to tower with letters 'ABCDE'—a school may have been held here; Royal Arms 1685; old bench ends; roodloft stairs; choir stalls; reliquary of SS Probus and Grace in sanctuary; stocks; tower details; niches, etc.

Guide

QUETHIOCK   D. St Hugh
(originally St Cadoc)

Present church—chancel, nave, north aisle and north transept, south transept, porch and west tower. Outlines of Norman cruciform church can still be traced, though rebuilt in 14th cent. North aisle added in 15th cent but did not wholly absorb north transept, which partly remains in shallower form. Slender and unique tower. Restored 1878–9. Old woodwork remains in roofs. Rev William Willimott, vicar 1878–88, restored this church, then largely ruinous, and enriched it with much carved oak of his own handiwork. All the stained glass was made by him in Quethiock, except one medieval fragment.

NOTE: Mutilated Norman font; unusual tower built on west gable; peculiar combined roodloft stair and squint; roofs; canopied recesses for effigies in both transepts; splendid brasses to Roger Kyngdon and family with sixteen children 1471, and Richard Chiverton, wife and eleven children 1631; slate memorial to Hugh Vashmond 1599; monument to Rev Obadiah Ghossip, 'outed' vicar during Commonwealth; carved furniture, painted panels and stained windows by Willimott— one saint has six fingers; churchyard cross discovered buried; organ good for small church, funds for which were collected by another vicar, Wix, selling walking sticks he made himself.

Guide

RAME   D. St Germanus

Present church—chancel, nave, south aisle, north transept, porch, tower with spire at west end. Norman church stood here, of which the tympanum and font base survive. Possibly some of the lower walling on the north side is of the same period, but there are 13th and 14th cent evidences in tower and chancel doorway and windows; south aisle is 15th cent with original roof. Restored 1848, 1886 by J. P. St Aubyn and furnished with Victorian woodwork, though some old woodwork remains in roofs and bench ends.

NOTE: Norman tympanum; tower and spire possibly of 13th cent date; piscinas in chancel, north transept and south aisle; roodloft stairs; squint; bench ends; good modern woodwork; screen; broomstick candle holders; 14th cent doorway erected at entrance to tower; organ in west gallery; cartoons of life of St Germanus; monument in north transept 1677; Jacobean altar rails; almsbox 1633; memorial ledger stones in aisles 17th cent, some to Plymouth merchants; one medieval bell (inaccessible); headstones in churchyard to coastguards, sailors, pilots, etc; snowdrops in spring worth seeing.

Rame Head is a 14th cent chapel of St Michael.

Guide

REDRUTH   D. St Euny
Present church—chancel, nave, north and south aisles, porch and west tower of three stages. Some evidence of a Norman church with apsidal chancel, traces of which were found in rebuilding 1756. Nave with two rows of Tuscan piers matched to late 15th cent tower of old church, some fragments of which survive. Much enriched since.
NOTE: Norman gargoyle and carved heads on tower; Tuscan arcades; coffered ceiling; memorials, including one with bust by Chantrey to William Davey 1827; part Celtic cross on window ledge; Georgian slate commandment tables; figure of St Euny in north aisle window; medieval lead crucifix; portrait of Rev John Collins, rector 1734–75, who knew Wesley well and was commended in the latter's 'Journal'; lychgate 1810 with pinnacles. The last public penance in Cornwall was observed here in 1834.

Guide

Redruth (D. St Andrew)
Present church—chancel, nave, north and south aisles, Lady chapel, porch and undercroft. Erected 1884 and completed 1938. Daughter church to above.

ROCHE

NOTE: Triple lancet east window, Christ reigning over town; standard candlesticks, old Cornish bedposts; Florentine stoup; Spanish sanctuary lamp, once property of Nelson's Lady Hamilton; painting in Lady chapel.

ROCHE   D. St Gonandus

Present church—chancel, nave, south aisle, north transept, porch and stately west tower of three stages. Norman font, similar to Bodmin but inferior in execution, and traces in northern walls show a Norman church once stood here. The old 15th cent south arcade was removed at the beginning of 19th cent and the building turned into an auditory. This was reversed in the restoration of 1890 when a new arcade, etc was erected on the old foundations. No old woodwork survives.

NOTE: Norman font; curious chalice-like stop at base of respond of transept arch; memorial windows; worked flat granite stone and fine ancient cross in churchyard; windows have no dripstones. Visit Roche rock, with hermitage and chapel.

ROCK, Porthilly. See under St Minver

RUAN LANYHORNE
                    D. St Rumon

Present church—chancel, nave, south transept and north aisle, porch and west tower of two stages. Possibly a Norman church stood here, of which south transept and chancel may preserve something of the cruciform shape. The north aisle is 15th cent. Tower 14th cent. Restored 1866. Some old woodwork is made up into lectern, pulpit, etc.

NOTE: Norman style font but possibly later in date; effigy of 13th cent priest; sedilia; credence; pulpit; squint, interesting; arms of Cambridge colleges painted above arches in roof; memorials; sundial 1743; Rev John Whitaker, rector 1778-1808 and historian, is buried under the altar.

RUAN MAJOR   D. St Rumon

Present church—chancel, nave, porch and low west tower. Restored drastically in 1866, the north aisle being removed and the arcade built up. Tower and font probably 15th cent. Now roofless and redundant.

NOTE: Tower with granite and serpentine chequered effect; 13th cent windows in south wall; font removed to Ruan Minor.

RUAN MINOR   D. St Rumon

Present church—chancel, nave, north aisle, porch and west tower of one stage, all on diminutive scale. Norman font, recut (?). Late 14th cent north aisle. Some 15th cent windows. Restored 1854. Modern woodwork.

NOTE: 13th cent font, or possibly Norman, recut; 13th cent piscina with star moulding; serpentine blocks in walls; low arcade; creeper covering tower especially attractive in autumn.

SALTASH   D. SS Nicholas and Faith

Present church—chancel, nave, north and south aisles, north chancel chapel, south transept, porch and tower of three stages on north side. There are clear traces of Norman building in tower base, doorway on south side (blocked) and perhaps lower parts of walls. Chancel chapel is possibly 14th cent. The arcades are 15th cent, as is porch. Restored in 19th cent and again, and enriched in 1930s. Old woodwork remains only in roofs.

NOTE: Font, from Wadgworthy in the parish, is probably a domestic quern; Norman doorway; Norman windows in chancel; arches in south transept; north-east chapel; curious piscina; organ peculiarly perched on iron columns in north aisle; clock in tower dates from about 1720, and is thus a rarity for Cornwall; memorials, especially to Drew brothers with ship plunging to wreck; communion plate (inaccessible) includes silver cup with cover from time of Henry VII; large stoup.

The church was a chapel-of-ease in which the corporation had rights. Made parochial 1881. It had a narrow escape during the war in 1943 when incendiary bombs penetrated the roof.

ST SAMPSON   D. St Sampson
  (or Golant)

Present church—chancel, nave, south aisle, porch and west tower. Wholly 16th cent building on earlier site. Ancient well by south door. Old roofs and woodwork remain. Roofs have inscriptions carved recording the guilds which provided them in 1509. An 18th cent flavour remains in chancel and nave, with box pews and communion rails of that time. Restored 1842. The fittings and furnishings of south aisle are modern.

NOTE: Old glass in north window of chancel; Royal Arms James II 1685; carved head of Christ, memorial to Rev J. Leycester Lyne (relative of the then vicar Charles Lyne), 'Father Ignatius of Llanthony', a famed Victorian preacher who pioneered the restoration of Benedictine monasticism in the Anglican church and who preached his first sermon here; box pews; traditionally, King Mark, Tristan and Iseult worshipped in the earlier church on this site.

SANCREED   D. St Credan

Present church—chancel, nave, 15th cent south aisle, north transept, porch and west tower of two stages. Fragments of a Norman font show a church of that date stood here in succession to a Celtic shrine, and itself gave way to 13th–15th cent structure, of which tower remains. Restored 1891. Old woodwork survives in screen and south aisle roof and one bench end.

NOTE: 14th cent font; small blocked priest's door to Lady chapel; piscina, almsbox dated 1739; lower part of screen with interesting panels and good modern completion and restoration; stoup; east window with scenes of local industry; sundial; interesting crosses in churchyard.

Guide

SENNEN   D. St Senana

Present church—chancel, nave, south aisle, north transept, porch and west tower of three stages. Cruciform 13th cent church with 15th cent south aisle. Restored 1867. Modern woodwork.

NOTE: Inscription on font base 1441, consecration of church; wall painting; pillars square with four half-round shafts, as St Veep; mutilated stone figure of Virgin in transept; roodloft stairs; candelabra, twelve lights; stone with legend in churchyard; old crosses.

Guide

SHEVIOCK   D. St Mary

Present church—chancel, nave, north aisle, south transept, porch and slender west tower with spire. Mostly 13th (tower) and 14th cent with especially fine five-light east window tracery with niches for statues, north aisle late 16th cent. Chancel restored 1851 (with much ecclesiastical ceremony, of which an account survives); and the rest 1872 by G. E. Street. There is old woodwork in the roofs and many bench ends.

NOTE: Font 13th cent; Courtenay effigies 14th cent; east window tracery; niches; sedilia; piscinas; roodloft stairs; heraldic glass in south window of chancel; monuments 16th and 17th cent; bench ends; seraphine (old musical instrument like harmonium 19th cent); stocks.

Guide

SITHNEY   D. St Sithney

Present church—chancel with aisles, nave, north and south aisles, north and south transepts, porch and west tower of three stages 15th cent. Two Norman stones in porch, and a font bowl of same date. Restored; old woodwork only in porch roof. Poor modern pulpit, etc.

NOTE: Norman font bowl; piscina with modern aumbry; stone coffin lid; old glass medallions 13th cent (?); memorials;

panelled and carved arches of tower and windows; pillar monument in churchyard designed by Rev William Borlase with epitaph written by Pope to parents of Dr Oliver, inventor of Bath Oliver biscuits, once much favoured; statue of St Sithney under pinnacle of tower wreathed on his feast day in August.

SOUTH HILL   D. St Sampson

Present church—chancel, nave, north transept, Manaton chapel with squint, 15th cent south aisle and porch, west tower of 14th cent. Probably cruciform in 14th cent. Norman building once here, of which font survives. Harshly restored 1871. Old woodwork still in roof of south aisle.

NOTE: Norman font; inscribed stone with Chi-Rho sign; piscinas; slate memorials to John Manaton 1507, Michael Hill 1663; Easter sepulchre; monuments; heads of apostles on tower.

SOUTH PETHERWIN
D. St Paternus

Present church—chancel, nave, north and south aisles, porches and west tower of three stages, oblong. Norman church stood here, of which the font and the north door remain, as well as a capital and reassembled pier in churchyard. There are traces of a Norman respond at junction of north arcade with tower. The building as it now stands is mostly 15th cent. Restored 1889 by G. Fellowes Prynne. Some old woodwork.

NOTE: Norman font; Norman north door spoiled by 16th cent arch; stoup on west side unique, being carved from solid; two 13th cent sepulchral slabs in tower; respond at west end of north aisle; 15th cent altar slab in south aisle chapel; 17th cent slate wall tablet with good lettering; Jacobean pulpit dated 1631; desk; old bench ends in choir stalls; pier and capital in churchyard; oblong tower; roodloft stairs; old woodwork in tower screen 1901; some old glass shields in south aisle window; Royal Arms James I.

ST STEPHEN-IN-BRANNEL
D. St Stephen

Present church—chancel, nave, north aisle, south chapel, porch and stately west tower of three stages. Norman survivals of font and south doorway show a church of that date stood here. Largely 15th cent, but south chapel possibly later. Restored 1854–71 by G. Fellowes Prynne, and again in 1893. Some old woodwork in north aisle roof, panels in desk and pulpit.

NOTE: Fine Norman font; Norman south doorway; baptistry and tower raised above church; old communion rails; piscina in chancel (used as aumbry); copper panel of crucifixion; memorial east window shows parish industries; sundial 1806; old cross and shaft in churchyard; note tower stair turret is chamfered off in unusual fashion instead of rising as a turret to parapet.

ST STEPHENS-BY-LAUNCESTON
D. St Stephen

Present church—chancel, north chancel chapel, nave, south aisle, north transept, porch with parvise and grand west tower of three stages 16th cent. Norman circular font is evidence of a church of that period and the northern wall of nave and chancel provide further traces of a probably cruciform shaped building. Alterations and enlargements in 14th and 15th cent. The mother church to Launceston and surrounding parishes. Restored 1883 by Hine and Odgers of Plymouth.

NOTE: Norman font; piscina; south door with 'sanctuary ring'; slate memorial to John and Anne Bewes 1675; 1883 pulpit with carved panel of stoning of St Stephen; traces of sacristy or Lady chapel at east end outside; stone coffin; carvings on east wall exterior of Romanesque period.

ST STEPHENS-BY-SALTASH
D. St Stephen

Present church—chancel, nave, north and south aisles, porch and tower of three stages at west end of north aisle, with turret

STOKE CLIMSLAND

in centre of north side and closed west door to tower. Norman survivals in font and lower part of tower. Mainly 15th cent. Restored 1872. Old woodwork in nave and aisle roofs.

NOTE: Fine Norman font of Bodmin type; coloured stone reredos; memorials; matrices of brasses; aperture in north arcade made to view preacher; slate table tomb memorial to Frances and William Hechins 1593; tomb with effigy c 1600; roodloft stairs; 'Armada' iron chest; early coffin slab with cross; copy Fox's *Book of Martyrs*; Royal Arms; sundial 1783.

STOKE CLIMSLAND
D. Unknown

Present church—chancel, with aisles, nave, north and south aisles, porch and stately 15th cent tower at west end. No Norman traces. The building is mostly 13th–15th cent work. The arcade to north aisle is granite, the south Polyphant. Restored 1860. Some old woodwork in roofs.

NOTE: Old font, recut; 14th cent piscina in chancel; roodloft stairs; memorials; slate memorial to Clare and Mary Manington 1605; John Bagwell, former rector, 1623, in vestry; Lady chapel curtains and frontal from material at Coronation of Elizabeth II; chandelier; sundial 1835.

Guide

STRATTON   D. St Andrew

Present church—chancel, nave, north and south aisles, porch and west tower of three stages. Norman church, whose foundations—including an apsidal chancel—were uncovered at the 19th cent restoration, stood here. 14th cent Polyphant north arcade, east part reconstructed, south aisle granite and 15th cent. Stone with date 1160 on west wall of north aisle. Old woodwork and many interesting features remain, and much good modern woodwork.

NOTE: Norman font; Polyphant piers in north arcade, and bases of piers revealed by lowering floor; 18th cent poor box; old

150

stocks; Jacobean pulpit; 33 good bench ends; relics of Civil
War battle nearby 1643; effigy 14th cent of Ralph Blanch-
minster; brass to Sir John Arundell 1572 (ask permission to
rub); Easter sepulchre in chancel north wall; bench ends;
Burne-Jones/Morris east window; old Clink (prison) door in
porch; old and new statues; contract exists (not available) for
making screens and benches 1531; modern slate carving of
Nativity; Guildford clock chimes (unusual) composed 1841;
cushions on ringers' seats representing course of bells in their
changes; modern statue on tower west front of St Andrew;
feature on west wall enclosing window and door.

Guide

STYTHIANS   D. St Stedyana
Present church—chancel, nave, north and south aisles, north
porch and stately tower of three stages at west end. Mostly 15th
cent (north aisle 14th) drastically restored in 1870s. No old
woodwork remains.
NOTE: Seats in side aisles ranged along walls; roodloft stairs;
brass tablet over rood doorway with 16th cent admonition;
piscina in chancel with old, possibly Norman, carved basin;
stained windows; memorials, one with Britannia and a Maori
warrior 1912; good panelled pulpit; augmented peal of bells to
six; new clock 1950.

Guide

TALLAND   D. St Tallanus (?)
Present church—chancel, nave, south aisle, north transept,
porch at west end with two entrances, leading also to detached
tower of three stages, partly built into the rock on the south
side. Possibly 13th cent, as there are three lancet windows in
west wall, but enlarged and reconstructed in 14th and 15th
cent. Much old woodwork of continuous period unspoiled by
religious changes in 16th cent.
NOTE: Wealth of splendid 15th and 16th cent benches; helmet

and cuirass of Bevill family; 13th cent lancet windows in west wall; slate memorials to John Bevill 1579 (tomb chest), Jane Mellow 1628, showing her in four-poster bed with her son; slate stone to Robert Mark, smuggler, shot at sea; parts of screen.

Polperro has a chapel-of-ease, St John's, erected 1837 with west gallery and clock of that date.

ST TEATH　　　　D. St Tetha

Present church—chancel, chancel aisles, nave, north and south aisles, porch, west tower of three stages, unbuttressed. Norman traces in junction of north arcade and tower, and tower base. Parts of Norman capitals remain in the church and could once have been a part of the structure. Aisles are 15th cent and granite. Restored 1877–9. Old woodwork in aisle roofs and bench ends. Modern screenwork as parcloses.

NOTE: Font 14th cent and cover with model Celtic cross; pulpit with panel dated 1630 and Cornish motto 'Cala rag Whetlow' (straw for a tale bearer); fragments of old glass; aumbry; tower west doorway 1630; roodloft stairs; pieces of carved Norman capitals; 14th cent effigy; good bench ends; niche in north chancel window; almsbox 17th cent with figures; slate memorial to Frances Bennett 1636; sundial 1836; tall ancient cross in churchyard. This church was once collegiate with several prebends, but was dissolved in 1545.

Delabole, St John's church, erected 1879, with chancel, nave, south aisle, south-western porch tower.

NOTE: slate altar front; use of slate in other furniture.

TEMPLE　　　　D. St Catherine

Present church—chancel, nave, north transept, porch and west tower, all 1883. A lonely church in the desolate moor. The Knights Templar had a commandery here in 12th cent. The church then built had become a ruin by 18th cent. An ash tree of some size grew in the nave. Rebuilding 1883 was wholly new except lower course and arch of tower. Font early Norman. After dissolution of the order the property fell to the Crown and was exempt from the bishop's jurisdiction. It became a kind of Gretna Green for illicit marriages. One tradition is that at one time the whole male population was hanged for sheep stealing. As there were only two men in the parish, this is not so dreadful. In 1771 a woman of this parish, Edith Galpin, was ordered to do public penance in the churches of Blisland and Cardinham for an offence against morals. This sentence of the archdeacon's court was duly carried out. The church is still used monthly in the summer.

NOTE: Fragments of old church set in walls of churchyard shed; cross in churchyard to Rev C. E. Lambert, who died on the moor after taking evensong; his faithful dog remained whimpering at his master's side for three days before the discovery of the body.

TIDEFORD D. St Luke

Present church—chancel and nave, with porch and bell gable, of 1845.

NOTE: Norman font, once in ruined chapel of St Luke in St Neot parish, brought here when church erected. Star pattern and corner heads.

TINTAGEL D. St Materiana

Present church—chancel, north chapel, nave, north and south transepts, porches and a west tower of three stages.

This church displays clearly the Norman or even earlier cruciform structure (which once possibly also had a central tower) and is of great interest as little alteration, except the western tower of 14th cent, obscures the original plan. The church was restored in 1870 by J. P. St Aubyn. Some old woodwork remains, and there is much evidence of later care and enrichment.

NOTE: All Norman features of this church—font with splayed

shafts; south doorway (note one shaft is circular, the other octagonal); earlier north door with original 14th cent iron work; north nave window of Norman date; 12th cent north chapel with original altar; piscina; niche in north transept; stone bench in south transept; bench ends (behind altar); roodscreen; stone coffin lid with floriated cross; brass of Joan Kelly c 1430 (ask permission to rub); 4th cent Roman inscribed stone; modern stained windows; 17th cent memorials; headstones in churchyard buttressed against gales.

TORPOINT   D. St James the Great
Present church—chancel, oblong nave with west gallery, west vestibule and bell turret. A plain Georgian preaching-box chapel-of-ease to Antony erected 1819, graced in late Victorian period with a chancel in 14th cent style. In 1930s north and south galleries were removed and complete and interesting transformation made under Sir Charles Nicholson. Damaged by blast in war, windows, etc replaced to same designs. Made parochial 1873.
NOTE: Good modern screenwork; renewed stained east window; organ in gallery, where the flute and the £5 cello of the church band of 1819 once sounded; sermon at opening in same year survives in MS, must have taken over an hour to deliver.

TOWEDNACK   D. St Tewennocus
Present church—chancel, nave, south aisle, porch and low west tower of two stages built of large granite blocks. The rare feature in Cornwall of a chancel arch appears here 13th cent. A Norman church is attested by the lower part of the font and north wall of nave; the tower is 14th cent, but most of the building 15th cent. South aisle and porch 18th cent. Restored 1870 by J. D. Sedding. Some old woodwork saved at that time, but previous restorations had destroyed all but some roof timbers and two bench ends dated 1633. A rare altar slab (?) early 11th cent may be Norman.
NOTE: Font, base Norman, bowl dated 1720; altar stone; bench

ends with 17th cent figures in hats; aumbry; odd layout of
tower stairs (cf Advent); incised stone in porch; great granite
slabs in walls.

Guide

TREGONY See under Cuby

TRELEIGH   D. St Stephen
Present church—apsidal chancel, nave, transepts, porch in a
14th cent style built about 1870.
NOTE: Stained glass in apse; decorative woodwork of roof;
well-kept churchyard, notable for primroses and daffodils.

TREMAINE   D. St Winwaloe
Present church—chancel, nave, porch and west tower of two
stages. Once merely a chapelry. The nave north wall and part
of south wall, the font and tympanum to blocked north door
are Norman. The tower is 14th cent and the porch probably
17th cent.
NOTE: Font; remains of Norman tympanum (with stove pipe
hole) over north door of same period; windows; cavity in north
wall once an Easter Sepulchre (?); old timber in roofs; modern
stone altar; recent careful restoration, in which rows of hat pegs
were removed from the walls.

Guide

TRENEGLOS   D. St Gregory
Present church—chancel, nave, north aisle, south porch and
tower at west end. A Norman building once stood here. Extensively restored in 1858 and tower rebuilt. All old woodwork
swept away except in porch roof.
NOTE: Norman font, bowl-shaped with four carvings at corner
of base; interesting Norman tympanum over south doorway,
with two beasts and a tree; roodloft stairs; woodwork in porch
roof; slate ledger stone depicting person in coffin; pulpit in

roodloft staircase, clerk's desk below; stocks; in 1847 the church-wardens were arraigned before the archdeacon for refusing to get the church linen washed.

TRESILLIAN   D. Holy Trinity

Present church—chancel, nave, south aisle, porch and bell gable with three bells. Chapel-of-ease to Merther, erected 1878, remodelled and consecrated 1904. This now replaces the old church at Merther, officially a ruin. The two bells, font, Jacobean pulpit and other details from Merther were brought here. The third bell is from Lamorran.

NOTE: Norman font; Jacobean pulpit; statue of St Anthony; modern arcade with peculiar springing of arches; part of stoup; one bell medieval, 15th cent; old cross in churchyard.

Merther (D. St Cohan) is now ruinous. It was 14th cent, chancel, nave, south aisle, porch, and west tower with wooden top stage. Piscina and niche in chancel; Victorian texts on walls, 'How dreadful is this place'; fireplace in south aisle (vestry?); remaining bell of three recast 1970 to augment St Clement's, Truro, to six.

TRESLOTHAN   D. St John the Evangelist

Present church—chancel, nave, porch, bell gable. Erected 1841 by George Wightwick, restored 1880. A previous church or chapel existed on this site or nearby.

NOTE: Font 15th cent, brought from Camborne, with four carved angels and a Latin inscription (cf St Winnow); alabaster panel of 'Adoration of Magi' in vestry, a gift; mausoleum of Pendarves family in churchyard.

TRESMERE   D. St Nicholas
(at reconsecration 1881)

Present church—chancel, nave, porch and tower at west end. Norman font, circular with triangular base. Traces of 13th cent windows. All rebuilt, except tower, about 1880.

NOTE: Norman font and curious base; stoup in porch; piscina in chancel; triple lancet east window; nave windows; part of churchyard cross set in porch wall; crosses in churchyard; two medieval bells 14th cent (inaccessible). Rev John Wesley preached several times in this church 1745–51.

TREVALGA   D. St Petroc

Present church—chancel, nave, north transept 13th cent; porch, west tower of three stages 13th and 15th cent. Norman church here, of which font and part of nave wall remain as evidence. Restored 1875. A few fragments of old woodwork survive, and there is good modern woodwork and furnishing.

NOTE: Norman font, circular; reredos in three panels, ancient; squint; granite bracket on east wall; piscina; memorials; ancient cross in churchyard; three bells, one medieval c 1400.

TREVERBYN   D. St Peter

Present church—chancel, nave, south porch and turret, erected 1850, G. E. Street architect.

NOTE: Memorial windows 19th cent.

TREWEN   D. St Michael

Present church—chancel, nave, north aisle, bell gable. Re-modelled in 15th cent from Norman church of which nothing remains except font. Restored 1863–4. No old woodwork.

NOTE: Norman font; 14th cent east window; internal stoup; bell c 1400; granite slab in churchyard 1596.

TRURO   D. St George

Present church—apsidal chancel, nave, north and south transepts, porch and west tower with buttresses. Lancet style. Erected 1855 from designs by Rev W. Haslam, the ecclesiologist vicar of Baldhu.

NOTE: Victorian attempt at 13th cent details; painting in apse of cathedrals of Truro and Zanzibar; good modern statue of St George; memorial windows; stations of cross by Italian artist; baldachino by local craftsman; hanging rood to commemorate centenary 1955.

TRURO   D. St John

Present church—apsidal chancel, nave, aisles with galleries over, baptistry at west end, turret with cupola. Erected 1827–8 as a chapel-of-ease to Kenwyn in an Italian style.

NOTE: Adaptation of style to usual layout; galleries and generous moulded woodwork; crucifix on outside west wall as war memorial, seldom without flowers; engraving in vestry of Rt Rev John Medley, curate 1831–8, first bishop of Fredericton 1845.

TRURO   D. St Mary

Present church—quasi-chancel and nave, west tower and spire. Original church consecrated 1259, and enlarged with late 15th and early 16th cent south aisle. A tower and spire erected 1769. It was then chancel, nave, north aisle of irregular shape, south aisle with elaborate carved surface to exterior, porch and west tower with spire (not the present one). In 1880 the new cathedral was begun, incorporating the old south aisle of the church, which is the only part still existing. It retains its character as a parochial church, and is joined to the cathedral proper as an extra choir aisle with skilful integration into the system of arches at that point. Many vistas are opened up in this way. A tower and copper-covered spire stand at the west end and contain the old bells and clock of 1851. The south aisle contains some relics from the old St Mary's. The whole has been carefully restored and enriched.

NOTE: Font—Victorian; inlaid pulpit c 1760; organ by Byfield given 1750; 17th cent memorial with effigies to Robartes family (north transept of cathedral); two effigies of unknown subject in crypt; memorial to Owen Phippen 1636, commemorating capture by Turks in 1627; good roof with modern bosses; tryptych at altar; windows, etc; carved stonework, niches and heraldic devices on exterior walls.

TRURO   D. The Cathedral Church of the
Blessed Virgin Mary in Truro

Foundation laid 1880. Architect J. L. Pearson. Building completed 1910 with erection of west towers. Style 13th and 14th cent with something of France or Brittany about it. Recent addition of chapter house in modern style harmonises well with this triumph of high Victorian architecture. Visitors should obtain the guide available and be prepared to spend time studying almost every detail; the 19th cent Church revival in Cornwall reached the peak of its attainments in the founding, furnishing and enrichment of this building, entirely by benefactions and gifts.

NOTE: in particular, in the shortest stay: great crossing under central tower; reredos; baptistry, memorial to Henry Martyn, missionary and martyr; vistas; St Mary's Aisle; terra cotta of Via Dolorosa; ranges and subjects of windows; pieta; woodwork of canons' stalls, with figures and names of Celtic saints; great organ by Willis; one pier of south arcade in granite, erected in the open long before the nave was attempted, as a vision for the future; west front, twin towers and symbolic and historic subjects in niches; chapter house. The communion and other vessels are sometimes shown and application should be made to the vergers.

TRURO   D. St Paul

Present church—chancel, with side chapel, nave, north and south aisles, porches and tower of three stages on south side. Crypt under east end. Originally built 1846 as a chapel-of-ease to St Clement. Made parochial 1865. Enlarged 1883 and subsequently, tower 1910. The interior as left by Edmund Sedding a good imitation of a large Cornish church, the taller piers of north arcade giving the impression of later and 15th cent erection. A screen in traditional style has had to be removed. Central altar 1970.

NOTE: Tower pinnacles are statues of Sir Richard Grenville of the *Revenge*, Sir John Eliot, Bishop Trelawney, the fourth being the stair turret; small piece of granite let into chancel-chapel respond shows crystalline cross; stone pulpit, similar to one at Egloshayle and said to be ancient; the base did duty as cricket stumps on St Clement Vicarage lawn for many years.

TUCKINGMILL   D. All Saints
Present church—chancel, nave, south aisle, porch and western tower by Hayward. Erected 1844 in Norman style.
NOTE: Font, with bowl of Norman period, given 1845 from Menadarva; stained windows in chancel 19th cent; new peal of eight bells recently hung; new side chapel 1972.

ST TUDY   D. St Tudy
Present church—chancel, nave, south aisle, north chapel, porch and west tower of three stages, unbuttressed. The font and other survivals show a Norman church stood here, probably on the site of a pre-Norman building. In the 15th cent extensive remodelling left the church substantially as it is. Restored 1873. Old woodwork remains in roofs. The 16th and 17th cent memorials are particularly fine.
NOTE: Coped stone in porch, pre-Norman with carving of cable and scrolls; Norman font, square with panelled sides; Norman carved corbel figure; hatchments; ancient funeral helmet; slate memorials with figures, parts of tomb chests: Humphry Nicoll 1597, Alice Reskymer 1563; monument with kneeling effigies to Anthony Nicholls, 1659; late 16th cent Flemish painting of Last Supper; 18th cent painting of Annunciation; locally made wrought iron candlesticks 1971; figure of Risen Christ; 18th cent tapestry reredos; individual photographs of men and women from village who served in World War I; stone roof to porch. Members of the Bligh (of the *Bounty*) family are buried here.

TYWARDREATH   D. St Andrew
Present church—chancel, nave, south aisle, north transept, porch and tower of three stages at west end. A few 14th and

15th cent features remain after rebuilding by Richard Coad in 1880. South aisle is 15th cent form, and the unbuttressed tower 15th cent.

NOTE: Tomb stone of Thomas Colyns (d 1539), last prior of Tywardreath priory (the ruins lie below the church in the valley); bench ends; pulpit with old woodwork; piscinas; reredos of alabaster; altar restored from fragments of original one; modern granite altar in Lady chapel; west window of south aisle has catherine wheel tracery; memorial in churchyard to Bishop Gott, third bishop of Truro; clock 1887; memorial to Robert Harris, parliament officer, 1655.

Tregaminion chapel-of-ease 1815, chancel, nave and porch. There are two ancient cross heads.

ST VEEP   D. SS Ciricus and Julitta
Present church—chancel, nave, north and south aisles, porch and west tower of two stages. Originally cruciform, the church was enlarged and rededicated 1336. Tower, south doorway and south arcade are of this date. The north arcade with floriated capitals is 15th cent, though the responds are of the earlier date. Tower has unusual corner buttresses. Restored 19th cent. All old woodwork swept away except five pews with carved bench ends in south aisle. A Tractarian vicar adorned the plain Georgian pulpit with cast-out roof carvings from Oxford colleges. The effect now is one of county simplicity.
NOTE: 14th cent font; pulpit with attached carving; squint from north aisle; north and south arcades, crudity of capitals in latter; old altar stone of pre-Reformation date; Royal Arms Charles II 1661; unique virgin ring of six bells, and account of their casting 'in the stillness of the night' 1770; memorial to Nicholas Avent, 1794, war surgeon; stocks; sundial; ashes of Eric Portman, actor, are interred in churchyard.

VERYAN   D. St Simphorian
Present church—chancel, nave, north aisle, south transept,

west and south porches and tower on south side at end of
transept. There seems to have been no Norman predecessor.
Mostly 13th cent, arcade 15th cent. Restored 1847–50. Little
of the old woodwork survives, but there are fragments of screen.
Good modern woodwork.

NOTE: Font, Norman style but probably later; transept window
13th cent; fragments of old woodwork; modern granite altar
in Lady chapel; model of barque 1936, memorial to those who
lost lives on coast; memorials, especially to members of Trist
family, who provided rectors of the parish and built the round
houses in the village.

Guide

WARBSTOW   D. St Werberga
Present church—chancel, nave, north aisle, porch 1601 and
west tower of two stages. Originally a Norman church, now
mostly 15th cent. Restored 1861, when the south transept was
removed. No old woodwork left.

NOTE: Norman square font; arch over one-light window in
chancel, partly Norman; good tracery in windows; little old
organ; niche and floriated doorway in porch.

WARLEGGAN   D. St Bartholomew
Present church—chancel, nave, south aisle, porch and low
west tower of two stages. The spire was destroyed 1818. Part
of north wall may be 13th cent. Arcade 15th cent. Severely
restored in 19th cent with shiny pitchpine and boarded ceiling.

NOTE: Plaster Royal Arms Charles II 1664; communion plate
includes interesting silver gilt chalice of Elizabethan date (not
available for view); cross in churchyard; slate memorial to
Richard Bere 1618. The last resident rector, Rev W. Densham,
achieved some notoriety by preaching in an empty church, the
pews of which he filled with cards containing the names of his
parishioners. His rectory was surrounded by high hedges and
barbed wire.

WEEK ST MARY D. St Mary

Present church—chancel, nave, north and south aisles, porch with parvise and tall western tower of three stages. A probable Norman church has left no traces, and the building is mainly 14th and 15th cent. The north aisle and an extension of the south aisle are 15th cent, the tower dates from 1543 and has three bands of carving round it. Restored 1876–81. Some old woodwork survives in the aisle roofs and part of screen.

NOTE: Linenfold panels of pulpit; roodloft stairs; colourful ornaments; chest; good modern woodwork; slate memorial to Humphrey Pethick 1663, with incised figure of angel drawn in one unbroken line; carved fragments in porch; sundial; carving of hounds in full cry on west face of tower; niche on south tower face.

WENDRON D. St Wendrona

Present church—chancel, nave, north transept, south aisle, fine battlemented porch and west tower of three stages 14th cent, buttressed diagonally. Once cruciform, enlarged in 15th cent. North side of nave and chancel and of transept may be 14th cent. Restored 1868. Good modern woodwork.

NOTE: 15th cent font; arched recess in wall of chancel, for effigy (?); brass to Warin Penhaluryk 1535, another 1580 (ask permission to rub); part of ancient screen; piscina; sedilia; roodloft stairs; corbel for screen support; stocks; ringers' rules; sundial 1770; 18th cent lychgate with room over; small arch from chancel to south aisle, with corbel for screen; incised stone; ancient cross in churchyard; a former vicar, Canon G. H. Doble, achieved lasting fame throughout Europe for researches on Celtic saints.

Guide

ST WENN D. St Wenna

Present church—chancel, nave, north and south aisles, porch and west tower. Mostly 15th cent. Restored drastically in 1868.

Arcades are of piers with unusual section. Tower was struck by lightning in 1663 and lost its upper stage.

NOTE: Font, possibly genuine, probably only mock-Norman; piers of arcades; lowest stage of tower with deeply-cut panels, quatrefoils and mouldings; oddly placed belfry window on west side of tower; sundial with punning inscription, 'Ye know not when'.

WERRINGTON D. St Martin

Present church—chancel, nave, north and south transepts, porch and western tower, flanked by two smaller replicas. An original 12th cent church, of which the font remains and which was no doubt refashioned at various times, was pulled down by a former squire so that he might enlarge his mansion. It stood next to the mansion. The new church erected 1742 in the present position. A chancel was built in the late 19th cent and the flat nave ceiling removed.

NOTE: Norman font from old church; flanking towers reputed to be a replica of old west end; niches with twelve apostles (?); room over south porch once open to the nave, either a family pew or an old minstrel's gallery; on exterior eastern wall 16th cent slate tombstone, sometimes thought to commemorate a nephew of Sir Francis Drake, once squire; ancient carving on east wall, meaning unknown.

WHITSTONE D. St Anne

Present church—chancel, nave, north and south aisles, south porch and western tower of three stages. The circular Norman font survives to show a church of that period stood here. The church was rebuilt in 15th cent, the tower again possibly in 1689, as that date is carved upon it. Restored 1881–2. Some old woodwork survives in south aisle roof, worked in with modern timber, and in the north aisle.

NOTE: Norman font; old woodwork in roofs; odd window between porch and south aisle; aumbry or stoup in priest's door in south aisle; early slate memorial to Rev John Cornishe, 1535; other 17th cent memorials; west window of tower has tracery cut from one piece of granite; old bench ends in seat in chancel; modern screen 1911; holy well in churchyard with niche and 14th cent statue of St Anne, the Virgin and Child.

A former rector, Richard Buvyle, died 1358 and remarkable and well attested cures took place at his grave. Another, William Score 1736–87, had a reputation as a ghost layer. Once a cottager complained his potatoes had been stolen. In church next Sunday Score told his congregation, 'I find the guilty man has a feather on his nose'. The involuntary movement of the culprit betrayed him. More recently the rectors have been members of the Kingdon family.

ST WINNOW   D. St Winnoc

Present church—chancel, nave, south aisle, porch and west tower of three stages, buttressed. Exquisitely situated on very edge of Fowey river. A large parish with daughter churches. Norman traces in northern walls of nave, transept and chancel. 13th cent window in nave and traces of others on outside walls. Norman arch to transept rebuilt 13th cent. South aisle, porch and tower 15th cent. Restored 19th cent with care. Much excellent woodwork remains, including screen (coving restored 1907), 33 bench ends 16th and 17th cent, Elizabethan pulpit, two windows of old glass c 1500, slate memorials with good lettering.

NOTE: 15th cent font, with inscription; screen c 1520, with 1907 coving and 1920 figures; 33 bench ends 16th and 17th cent, one with ship, another with man in Cornish kilt; ancient glass in east windows; pulpit c 1590; anagram slate memorial to William Sawle: 'I WAS ILL AM WELL'; old chest; Jacobean table; part of sundial in vestry; memorials to Admiral Sir Charles Vinicombe Penrose and to Lieut Melville, hero of South African War; small modern brass.

There is an ancient chapel or daughter church, once quasi-parochial:

WITHIEL

St Nectan's Chapel (D. St Nectan or Nighton)
Present chapel—chancel, nave, porch, base of massive west tower. Existed 1250, but largely 15th cent. Medieval chapel may have had a small north aisle. In August 1644 the campaign of the Civil War round Lostwithiel and Boconnoc destroyed the upper stages of the tower and the building lay semi-desolate for some time. In 1825 the building was extended with cast iron arcade and a chancel erected 1864. This had become ruinous by 1947 and the building was closed. In 1971 the extension was removed and the 15th cent south aisle retained and restored. Old woodwork in porch roof.

NOTE: Font; tower arch; porch with old woodwork and good doorways; one old window on south side; tablets to memory of sisters of St Faith's Home; old cross in churchyard; pinnacle of old tower and other carved stones at entrance.

Bridgend has a chapel-of-ease, St Saviour's, Victorian with apsidal chancel.

Respryn, the site of a medieval chapel dedicated to St Martin. Some worked stones and traces of the old chapel are to be seen near the farm entrance near Respryn bridge.

WITHIEL   D. St Clement

Present church—chancel, nave, north and south aisles, porch and stately west tower of three stages. A Norman church stood here, but only the font base remains. The building is now mostly 15th cent. The narrow north aisle has a lean-to roof and is shorter than the length of the nave. It was the chapel of the lords of Brynn, the Bevills. Restored, no old woodwork remaining except in south aisle roof.

NOTE: Font with anchor, symbol of St Clement; old south aisle roof; painted slate altar piece behind organ; stoup with angel holding a shield; Georgian clear square panes; roodloft stairs opening, giving access to pulpit; relics of Victorian family pew in north aisle; pinnacles of chancel gable in 18th cent style.

The great Prior Vyvyan held the living 1522–33; Tudor rectory adjoining church.

ZENNOR   D. St Senara

Present church—chancel, nave, north aisle, south transept, porch and west tower of three stages, unbuttressed. Of the Norman church which stood here there are slight traces in a window and part of font. Mostly 15th cent. Restored 1890. Some old woodwork remains, and there has been later enrichment.

NOTE: Norman window near porch; piscina possibly also Norman; part of font; bench ends on chancel seat, one with the famous mermaid; niche above west window; figure of St Christopher; two medieval bells (inaccessible); sundial 1737; old crosses in churchyard; niche on west face of tower; Henry Quick the poet was born, lived and died here.

Guide

Glossary

AISLE: The subsidiary longitudinal portions of a church north and south of the arcades.

APSE: A semi-circular or many-sided end to a church.

ARCADE: A series of arches supported by columns or piers.

AUMBRY: A recess or cupboard in the wall of chancel or aisle for the safe keeping of vessels.

BATTLEMENT: Rectangular projections and indentations along the upper edge of a parapet.

BUTTRESS: An extra thickness of masonry built out from a wall to strengthen it.

CAPITAL: The overhanging uppermost stone of a pier which gives support to the springing of the arches above it.

CHANCEL: The part of the church containing the altar and choir.

CHANTRY: A chapel endowed for the saying of masses for the souls of departed parishioners.

CLERESTORY: Main walls supported by the arcades rising above the lean-to aisle roofs and pierced by windows.

CORBEL: A block of stone projecting from a wall to support a superimposed weight such as a parapet or wooden structure.

EASTER SEPULCHRE: A recess in the north wall of the chancel used in the ceremonial of Holy Week.

ECCLESIOLOGY: Study of the surroundings and requirements of worship.

GROIN: When arched surfaces, eg of the underside of porch or tower ceilings, intersect, the lines of meeting are often ribbed or 'groined'.

168

HOOD MOULDING, or DRIPSTONE: A projecting and protecting moulding around the exterior arch of a window etc, to help the rain run off.

JAMBS: The upright sides of a window or door opening.

LANCET WINDOW: Narrow window with a curved pointed top, so named from its likeness to the blade of a lancet.

MULLIONS: The vertical members dividing a window, supporting the tracery in the upper part.

NAVE: The main body of the church where the people congregate.

OGHAM: A peculiar kind of primitive 'writing' involving the cutting of inclined lines along the edges of stone.

PARAPET: The part of an exterior wall rising above the eaves of a roof.

PARCLOSE: A screen dividing a chapel or aisle from the body of the church.

PARVISE: The upper room over a porch, used for storing material or sometimes for the lodging of the priest in medieval days.

PIER: A column supporting the arches of an arcade. The section may vary from circular to a cluster of minor shafts.

PINNACLE: A tapering finish to a short column or similar feature on a wall or corner of a tower.

PISCINA: A niche in the wall south of an altar, containing a basin and drain hole for the washing of the vessels used in the service.

POUPEE HEAD: Poppy head. A carved termination to a choir stall or bench end; sometimes, for example, a crouched beast or symbolic figure.

QUOIN: Squared stones forming the angles of walls.

RESPOND: The half column or corbel taking the support of the last arch in an arcade where it meets the wall terminating it.

ROODLOFT: The gallery along the top of the roodscreen, which supports the statues and crucifix.

SEDILIA: Seats recessed into the wall south of the altar for the convenience of the priest during a long service.

GLOSSARY

SHAFT: A minor column.

SPANDREL: The triangular space of wall above the piers and between the arches of an arcade.

SQUINT: An opening in a wall or pier to allow a view of the main or high altar.

STOUP: A basin of stone for holy water at or near the entrance door.

TRACERY: Ornamental stone forming the shapings of the openings at the top of the windows.

TRACTARIAN: So-called from the 'Tracts for the Times' of 1833 onwards. Clergy and others who from the study of church principles found a new concern with the surroundings of worship and awakened in a wider public an enthusiasm for church restoration in the 1860s and '70s.

TRANSEPTS: The transverse parts of a church projecting north and south across the main axis.

TYMPANUM: The semi-circular space between the arch of a doorway and the horizontal line of the door itself. Often filled with sculptured ornament.

Bibliography

Betjeman, J. *Cornwall* (Shell Guide), Faber, 1964

Bizley, A. C. *Slate Figures of Cornwall*, Worden, Penzance, 1965

Blight, J. T. *Churches of West Cornwall*, Parker, 1865

Brown, H. M. *The Church in Cornwall*, Blackford, Truro, 1964

Cox, J. C. *County Churches—Cornwall*, Allen, 1912

Cox, J. C. & Ford, C. B. *Parish Churches of England*, Batsford, 1935

Doble, G. H. *The Saints of Cornwall.* Reprints in 6 parts, continuing

Henderson, C. H. *Cornish Church Guide*, Blackford, Truro, 1925

Pevsner, N. *The Buildings of England—Cornwall*, Penguin, Harmondsworth, 1951

Sedding, E. *Norman Architecture in Cornwall*, Ward, 1909

Index

Where items indexed below are to be found in several parishes, only a few of the better examples have been chosen, and any outstanding ones printed in bold type. Page numbers refer to general comment on the items concerned; the items without page numbers are mentioned in the main alphabetical sequence, pp 55–167.

172